Live Wire

Live Wire
BON SCOTT

A MEMOIR BY THREE OF THE PEOPLE WHO KNEW HIM BEST

MARY RENSHAW, JOHN D'ARCY AND GABBY D'ARCY

ALLEN&UNWIN
SYDNEY • MELBOURNE • AUCKLAND • LONDON

Allen & Unwin
83 Alexander Street
Crows Nest NSW 2065
Australia
Phone: (61 2) 8425 0100
Email: info@allenandunwin.com
Web: www.allenandunwin.com

Cataloguing-in-Publication details are available
from the National Library of Australia
www.trove.nla.gov.au

ISBN 978 1 76029 411 3

Set in 12.5/17 pt Minion Pro by Bookhouse, Sydney

10 9 8 7 6 5 4 3 2 1

For Bon, our friend

Foreword

By Michael Gudinski

It's funny, before I even knew that Darce, Gab and Mary were putting together this book, I'd been thinking a lot about Bon Scott.

It's stating the obvious to say that Bon was a figure of influence. It's amazing the number of international acts, all of different generations, that I bring in to tour Australia who want to go over to Fremantle while they're here to pay homage to Bon. And with the amount of travelling that I do, I've seen the 'Cult of Bon' develop and grow over the years, particularly in Europe and the States. Perhaps even more so than here in Australia—and we love the bloke!

What a lot of people don't know is how hugely important Bon has been to me personally. And not the denim-clad, wild-eyed Bon we all know from AC/DC, but the teenybopper-focused co-lead singer of The Valentines in the late sixties. This Bon wore orange frilly shirts and sang 'bubblegum' pop tunes like 'My Old Man's A Groovy Old Man', which is bizarre when you think about it. Mind you, though, his eyes could still get pretty wild.

As a kid around Caulfield I'd already started putting on a few dances—it was easiest during school holidays—and I ended up working for Bill Joseph, who was the manager of The Valentines. Bill was one of Melbourne's leading promoters at the time and he had a couple of nightclubs as well, and he took me under his wing.

I was pretty green, had never seen any of the rock'n'roll lifestyle—I was still a virgin and had never seen drugs. I was a clean-cut, straight-down-the-line sort of kid.

The Valentines were scheduled to tour Adelaide and I decided to tag along to get an idea of what actually happened on the road. It wasn't that hard to get permission—I'd already dropped out of school and been kicked out of home. Nothing could've prepared me for what ensued, though—that first taste of the rock'n'roll life.

Let's just say it opened my eyes.

I can't remember how we actually got to Adelaide but I do recall having to come home on a bus with the band—whatever the local equivalent of Greyhound buses was at the time. I wasn't a fan of a road trip at the best of times, and going all the way from Adelaide to Melbourne with a bunch of long-haired yahoos like The Valentines was certainly a colourful and testing time. I wouldn't say it was a particular highlight, but it left an indelible mark. We stayed at the Powell's Court Motel, in Adelaide, which would become well known as a place for bands to stay in years to come. I will never forget one night when Bon, after spending some time with a particularly enthusiastic groupie, showed me his bed sheets and started cracking jokes so impressively off colour that I can't bring myself to repeat them now.

I don't think I've been the same since.

There's no way I would've signed The Valentines if I'd had Mushroom Records in the late sixties. They were good, but a product of their time, pumping out bubblegum pop to screaming teenage girls. Ultimately, Bon got sick of the lightweight pop stuff and joined Fraternity, which was a band I really did like. They were a 'serious musician's' group, and gave Bon the cred he needed for the Young brothers to take notice.

I put Bon up as one of the most important music figures this country has produced. If not for a stupid tragedy, he would've hit the heights of another tragic figure—Michael Hutchence. To continue the theme, he would've been Australia's Jim Morrison.

Bon's death was devastating. He and I had kept in touch through the years as both our lives started to blow up. 'My, haven't you done well for yourself,' Bon would joke. To him, I was still the sixteen-year-old kid he tried to get to smoke hash on a trip to Adelaide—and shock with his bed sheets. For the record, I never succumbed to his influence and didn't muck up for the entire tour. Bon had a spirit that flowed onto the people he was with and I always enjoyed catching up, even if it did used to leave me a little worse for wear.

One thing I'll never forget about Bon is that cheeky glint in his eye. He could be cocky and a little pushy in his pursuit of a good time, but never aggressive. People seemed to get the wrong impression with the whole denim-vest-and-tattoos thing during the early AC/DC era.

Bon was simply a really decent bloke. He was a 'bloke's bloke', he liked to party, have fun, pull pranks, and he had this amazingly powerful voice. There was a song he'd written in The Valentines called 'Juliette', and if you listen back to it you can hear—behind all the orange and the frills—the voice that was the key factor in what would take AC/DC from what they were before, to what they would become.

I actually live not too far from where The Valentines shared a flat on Toorak Road in South Yarra, and I still think about Bon and those days when I drive by. Music is big business nowadays, but back then it was a different world. It was liberated and free: dictated by energy and adventure rather than commerce. The usual deal was one band, one roadie and three gigs a day, and a real sense of camaraderie built up around the group and the little community around it—people like Darce, Gab and Mary. I've bailed Darce out of jail, given him and Gab a place to have their wedding, and an old business partner of mine managed Mary's brother's band. At one stage we all had neighbouring shops in Greville Street, Prahran. These are the people and the times that informed a lot of my early life decisions. If I hadn't taken a four- or five-day trip to Adelaide I might never have got into the music business. That's how important Bon and these other guys are to me, so you can understand why I still think about them a bit.

It's great that Mary, Gab and Darce are now sharing their memories of a unique time in Australian music and a very special bloke. I hope you enjoy them, they mean a lot to me.

Contents

Introduction

By Mary, Darce and Gabby

There is no such thing as 'the definitive Bon Scott book'.

'You'd need several volumes of *Britannica*,' Angus Young once noted in *Rolling Stone*, 'just to chronicle what Bon got up to in one day.'

Bon had a lust for life. As his old Valentines' bandmate Vince Lovegrove observed, 'To Bon, success meant one thing—*more*. More booze, more women, more dope, more energy, more rock'n'roll . . . more life!' He was a guy who never needed any instructions for how to live his life. He just did it.

Only one man could have written the definitive Bon Scott book, and, sadly, he's no longer with us, though we doubt that the book would have happened—Bon would have been too busy living his life to sit down and reflect.

That said, Bon was a brilliant writer. He called it 'toilet poetry'. If you're reading this, you are most likely familiar with his AC/DC lyrics. He was the street poet laureate, the king of the double entendre, capable of coming up with killer rhyming couplets that could be both bawdy and philosophical. But you might be surprised to know that Bon was also a prolific letter writer. The letters are what kept us together. He lived a true rock'n'roll life, but amid the gigs, the girls and the partying, Bon always found time to keep in touch with his friends and family. No matter where Bon was in the world, he would always pen a lengthy letter. They were informative, funny, honest and sometimes crass—just like the man himself.

Much has been written about Bon's time with AC/DC; his days before that are a little more mysterious. Hopefully this book will fill in some of the gaps.

It's an amazing musical journey, from the bubblegum pop of The Valentines to the progressive rock of Fraternity and the classic Australian rock of AC/DC. As well as Bon's journey, this is the tale of his beloved bandmates and contemporaries, Australia's rock'n'roll pioneers. It really was a long way to the top. In some ways, it was a more innocent time—not that you could ever use the word 'innocent' to describe Bon!

This is also very much a personal story, about an unforgettable character who wanted to take his music to the world—and have a wild time doing it.

A lot of stories have been written about Bon; many of them are crap. Forget the myth, we were lucky enough to know—and love—the man. And these are our memories.

Headfirst

Mary

When I was young, my older brother had to look after me during the school holidays because both our parents worked. During the summer holidays we would always go to the Footscray Baths in the western suburbs of Melbourne.

The swimming pool had a high diving board. For a little kid, it looked terrifying, rising metres above the pool. Only adults dared to dive from the high board. But on this day I looked up to find a boy standing on top of it. He looked about my brother's age—nine.

I remember watching the boy through my five-year-old eyes, thinking he was a hero. What was he doing? Would he jump? Or would he chicken out? I stood at the shallow end, transfixed. It was as if the boy was waiting for a bigger audience. He stood on top of the board, looking around, seemingly wanting everyone to notice him.

And then . . .

He jumped.

I later found out that the boy's name was Bon Scott.

The job interview

Darce

I'd been off the road for a few months and was thinking that my rock'n'roll career might be over. After I'd worked as a roadie for New Zealand band Compulsion for five months, the guys decided to split. I returned to the gym and my boxing career. I was a nineteen-year-old flyweight. I had six fights in three months—three on the telly—then I got a call from my old mate Paddy Beach, who had been the drummer in Compulsion.

'Hey,' Paddy said, 'we need someone to look after us. I'm with this band, The Valentines. They're a teenybopper band.'

Gee, I thought, *that's a little strange.* Compulsion had been a heavy, Hendrix-inspired band, definitely not teenybopper.

'If you want to come on the road with us,' Paddy added, 'come and check it out and see what you think.'

I was living in the northern suburbs, so I whipped over to the other side of town, to a block of flats on Toorak Road, South Yarra, just down from Williams Road. There were three blocks of flats together. The Valentines were in the middle, on the second—and top—floor. Johnny Farnham was living at the back of the other block of flats, and Johnny Young was on the other side.

I knocked on the door of The Valentines' flat, and singer Vince Lovegrove greeted me. I walked into the lounge room, where I saw five guys I'd never met. Paddy was the only one I knew.

All the guys were checking me out. I was small, like Paddy. The band's other lead singer, Bon Scott, was a little bigger than me; the others were all much bigger.

They told me they had just bought new amplifiers and asked if I'd be able to handle their equipment. 'Well,' I said, 'all I can do is give it a go and we'll see what happens.'

Then, after I'd been there about thirty minutes, Bon remarked, 'Do you feel like a fuck?'

I wasn't quite sure what he meant. I looked him in the eye and casually replied, 'I could always go a fuck.'

'There's a young girl in that room there,' Bon smiled. 'She'll sort you out.'

I had no idea what was going on. Was this some sort of prank or strange initiation?

I walked to the room, opened the door and, sure enough, there was a young chick in there. Within a few minutes, I was lying on my back, the chick was going down on me, and Bon was doing her from behind.

I looked up to find a couple of the band members sitting on the bed, now starkers. 'How do you think you'll go?' one of them asked.

'Well, I'll try to adapt.'

After the job interview was done, I pulled on my jeans and

walked downstairs. Standing on Toorak Road, I scratched my head. *Did all that just happen?*

I had a job, I was moving in with the band, and I'd just been blown.

I raced back to the northern suburbs, packed up my stuff as quickly as I could, and returned to the Toorak Road flat.

So started two years of madness. My life would never be the same again.

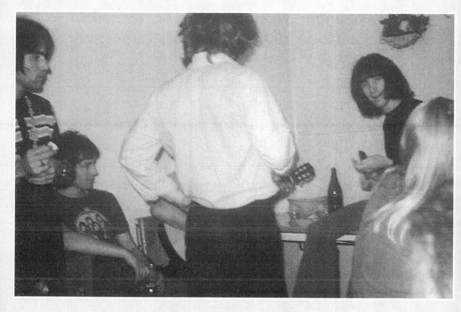

Soon after joining The Valentines—
this is at a party to send off original drummer Doug Lavery.
From left: Paddy Beach, Darce, Doug (back to camera). Bon's rolling a joint.

The fan

Gabby

I went to Caulfield High School, in the south-eastern suburbs of Melbourne. A school friend of mine knew a girl named Betty King, who went to another school. Betty and I hit it off and we dumped the other girl. From that point, it was Betty and me all the time. We used to wag school and go to see our favourite band, The Valentines. Well, they were Betty's favourite band, so they became my favourite band as well.

Betty was madly in love with one of the singers, Vince. I was just excited to be hanging out with a rock band.

One day, there was a knock on the door of the band's Toorak Road flat. It was my Mum. She came in and lectured the band.

'This is my daughter,' she said, pointing at me. 'She's fourteen. That's her friend, she's also fourteen. Thank you so much for looking after them.'

Then she added: 'I know where you live.'

It was Mum's way of saying, *She's in your hands.* And from that day on, Betty and I were under the protection of the boys in the band. They would make sure that nothing bad happened to us.

Gabby at home with a poster of her favourite band!

Gabby and Betty King at the flat at Toorak Road.
Gab: 'Note the ice-cream—this is how innocent we were!'

Love at first feel

Mary

My real name is Swetlana Wasylyk, but when I was born, an Australian friend pointed out to my parents that Aussies would never be able to pronounce that, so I took her name—Mary.

My parents, Stephan and Valentina, were Ukrainian; they met at a German work camp during World War II. Dad was a crafty, charismatic man who survived by selling things on the black market. He was a hero to my Mum—she was one of the few Ukrainian women at the time who got to wear a wedding dress on her wedding day.

My brother, Michael, was born in Germany in 1946. My Dad helped another family flee with a forged passport after the war, which left him worried that the Russians would find him. When Dad was asked which country he would like to settle in, he said Australia—as far away from Russia as possible.

After coming to Australia on a boat, my parents and brother were sent to the refugee camp at Bonegilla, in Victoria, not far from the New South Wales border. After about a month, my father—along with his family—was sent to Maldon, a Victorian gold-rush town, where he helped build the Cairn Curran Reservoir. I was born in Maldon in October 1950, and we stayed there until the mid-1950s, when we moved to Brooklyn, a western Melbourne suburb where lots of Ukrainian people lived. Initially, we stayed in a bungalow at a friend's house, and then the Ukrainian community banded together to build us a new home.

Mum and Dad both worked, so I was very independent from a young age. I would catch the bus to go to dancing school in Footscray. And I spent my spare time designing clothes for my Barbie Dolls. My brother learned guitar and played in a few bands. One of them even played on the TV show *Uptight* alongside a band called The Valentines. My brother's band was managed by Gavin Hogben, who was in partnership with a young guy named Michael Gudinski.

I couldn't play an instrument or hold a tune, but I loved music. In 1964 when The Beatles came to Melbourne, I wagged school to try to find them. I loved Paul. We heard that the band was going to the Melbourne Zoo, so that's where I headed, with two school friends. We saw some beetles but no Beatles, and we got into big trouble when our parents found out.

Unfortunately, I didn't get to see The Beatles at Festival Hall, because my brother was unable to get tickets, but he did get us tickets to see The Rolling Stones' first Melbourne show, at the Palais in 1965. It was one of the most astonishing things I'd ever seen. I loved seeing the support acts—Roy Orbison, The Newbeats, Ray Columbus & The Invaders and The Flies—and I'll never forget seeing Mick Jagger, in his tight white pants, shimmying across the stage.

I had caught the music bug.

Problem child

Darce

My old man busted my hand when I was ten. He stomped on it because I threw a punch at him. My Dad was one of the Rats of Tobruk and he came home from the war a troubled man. He used to beat my Mum and then he'd beat me when I tried to protect her. So, I was used to violence.

When I was a kid, I did a milk run at night, on a horse and cart. Often, I'd be stuck with a grumpy old bloke named Pop—he'd work me like crazy and then give me just two bob for my effort. Pop's last delivery was always to a woman. Given the amount of time he spent inside the house, he was obviously delivering more than milk. I got sick of Pop ripping me off, so one night I didn't do the run—instead I waited in a tree outside the woman's house. I knew where Pop kept his change, so when he went inside, I jumped out of the tree and stole Pop's cream bottle filled with coins.

I grew up in Pascoe Vale South, a northern suburb of Melbourne, and my parents sent me to the local Christian Brothers' school, St Joseph's College, hoping that the Brothers would straighten me out. It didn't work. The other kids would make fun of my second-hand books and uniform, so I'd beat them up. The only kid I connected with was Chris Flannery, who later became a notorious hitman known as Mr Rent-A-Kill. I was always getting the strap at school, but one day I decided I'd had enough: I grabbed the strap out of the Brother's hands, walked out of his office and threw the strap in the incinerator. I was thirteen.

I ended up in a boys' home, Turana, in Royal Park, where some of my new friends tried to bash me on my first day. I responded by holding one guy's head in the toilet until we were alerted by the cry of 'Screws!' No one bothered me after that. I was meant to spend six months in Turana, but I was struck down by bronchitis and asthma because my cell had a broken window and it was a bitterly cold Melbourne winter. I finished my last month in style—at the Royal Melbourne Hospital.

I've always been known as Darcy or Darce. Only my Mum or the police called me by my real first name, John. If I'm called John, I know I'm in trouble.

When I got out of the boys' home, I spent a lot of time at pool halls and gyms. If I won money playing pool, I would pay to get into the Friday night dance at the Ukrainian Hall in Essendon, seeing acts such as The Strangers, The Cherokees, Johnny Chester and Merv Benton. If I lost, I would jump over the back fence and gain entry that way, which often meant a punch-up with the bouncers.

They say there's one fuckwit in every family—well, in our family it was me. By the time I was sixteen, I was carrying a gun. My life was not going to turn out well. At seventeen,

I was living on the streets of Sydney. I remember standing on the corner of Darlinghurst Road and William Street in Kings Cross, watching Billy Thorpe drive by in his Aston Martin.

That was the life I wanted.

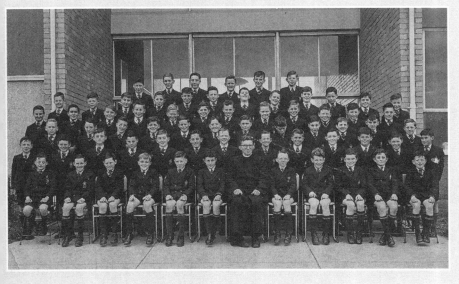

Class photo at St Joseph's College.
Also in the photo is Chris Flannery, who went on to become Mr Rent-A-Kill.
Darce is bottom left and Chris is fourth along from the left.

Darce: 'I'm the only kid with his feet off the ground, going cross-eyed. Definitely a problem child!'

Let there be rock

Gabby

My father, John Perry, was a war correspondent. He was British; you could have called him a stuck-up Pom. AC/DC released an album called *Stiff Upper Lip* and that's how you could describe my Dad: he was conservative and utterly correct. He married my mother, Lena, who was Maltese, in Malta, and then they lived in London. Five children later, they decided to move to Australia, where Dad got a job at *The Herald*. After twelve months, he said, 'See you later'—and suddenly my mother was a single mum.

She was forced to get a job, and my grandmother came from Malta to look after us. This was a big sacrifice for my Nanna—she had come from a well-to-do Maltese family, where she had servants to cook and clean, and she gave all that up to move thousands of miles away to look after five kids. I remember her complaining, 'I've come here to be your maid—I've never swept a floor in my life!' My little brother, Mark, innocently and helpfully replied: 'It's easy, Nanna—you just put the broom down and you walk.'

My Mum had run ballet schools in Malta and London, so she started teaching dance in Melbourne. I studied ballet for many years, and I probably could have got a scholarship with the Australian Ballet—but instead I discovered rock'n'roll and broke my mother's heart.

As for Dad, well, he never returned. I was born on his birthday, but not once did he send me a card or a present on our shared day. I saw him only once after he ran out on us. When I was sixteen, my two older sisters tracked him down—he was living with his new wife in Perth—and organised to meet him in the city. 'Dad's coming to Melbourne,' they told me. 'Come and see him.'

I went to where they were meeting, but Dad had just left. As I walked down the road, I saw him standing at the traffic lights, so I approached him and tapped him on the shoulder.

'Oh, it's jolly good to see you,' he said. Looking me up and down, he added, 'I didn't think you'd turn out like this.' My sisters had told him that I was running around with bands, and I think he was expecting to see some sort of wild child and not the well-presented young woman standing in front of him. By this stage in my life, even though I was only sixteen I was already living with Darce and working at the In Shoppe, a very groovy fashion outlet in the city, where I was an assistant to the designer of the Clementine label, Dawn Klingberg (who was also an actress and later appeared in *Prisoner*, and the movies *One Perfect Day* and *Innocence*).

When our first child, Rebecca, was born a few years later, Dad sent a telegram to the hospital congratulating me.

In 1980, we had planned a trip to Sydney for a wedding and I knew that Dad was working there as a journalist. Now that I was a mum, I knew I was ready to see him. I rang the newspaper where Dad was working. 'Oh,' said the woman on the phone, 'I'm very sorry but he died.'

One of my brothers got a copy of Dad's death certificate. It listed just two children. And the woman he was living with knew none of his history. But did we miss out on anything? No. We were lucky to be raised by two wonderful, strong women. And if I needed positive male role models in my life, I had Darcy and the boys in the band. Sure, they had a wild side—it was sex, drugs and rock'n'roll. But they were also my protectors, always looking out for me, like a big brother would.

'He had one of my false nails stuck on his bum!'

Mary

I had always wanted to work in fashion, and when I was sixteen I left school to work at Norma Tullo, one of the biggest fashion houses in Melbourne. Norma was pretty traditional, but she made beautiful, expensive clothing. I was working in the basement, where all the stock came in. I'd pack it up and it would be sent to shops around Australia. I was also sending sketches to Norma Tullo because I wanted to be a fashion designer and hoped she could help me start my career.

It was a sociable workplace with many girls my age and we'd often go to 10th Avenue, a venue in Bourke Street that held lunchtime rock shows. It was the most wonderful thing; I don't know why they don't do it nowadays. During our lunch hour, we'd see bands such as The Easybeats, The Wild Cherries, The Purple Hearts and The Loved Ones. A real scene was developing in Melbourne, involving music and fashion, and I loved being a part of it. It was such a fun, happy atmosphere. *'What am I doing? I'm going to see a band!'*

I remember spotting the footballer Carl Ditterich at 10th Avenue. Being a St Kilda supporter, I had a big crush on the big, blond ruckman. I flashed him a smile and said hello, but that was it; I was too shy for anything else.

It was a cool place to be. We'd climb the stairs and be in a groovy little club, holding no more than a hundred people. We could only buy soft drinks, but that didn't worry us; we were just happy being part of the scene. We would also frequent another great little venue, The Bowl, beneath a bowling alley in Degraves Street, near Flinders Street Station.

When Norma Tullo moved to Richmond, I stayed in the city and got a job as a designer at Kenneth Pirrie, where we designed knitwear, evening wear, daywear and lingerie. It was 1968; I'd just turned eighteen and I was a fashion designer. Life was good. Then I went to see a band called The Valentines at 10th Avenue. A friend had seen them and she was a fan. After the show, one of the singers came up to me and started chatting. He was admiring the beads I was wearing, or, at least, that's what he claimed. As he stared at my beads, he asked if I could make him some.

'Sure,' I said. 'What's your name?'

'Bon,' he smiled. 'Bon Scott.'

And that was it; we were friends from that day on.

As well as the hippie beads, I made Bon a velvet bolero. With jewels and gold braid, it was very Jimi Hendrix.

I became a regular at The Valentines' gigs. They were singing mostly covers, but they had a great dynamic on stage and their shows were always fun. Rock'n'roll bands were such a new thing in Australia and it was exciting to hang out with one.

I remember at one show Bon was struggling to sing because he had a dry throat. 'Can someone get me a Coca-Cola?' he requested, but no one did. Then, gasping for air, he added, 'I really need a Coca-Cola!' so I rushed off to get him a drink. After the show, Bon revealed that he suffered from asthma, though it never seemed to affect his singing career.

I also started visiting the band at their house, an old double-storey place in Dalgety Street, St Kilda. A lot of musicians lived in the area because it was cheap. St Kilda in the late sixties was also quite edgy; there were a lot of boarding houses and working girls in the area. Bon's co-lead singer, Vince Lovegrove, had the front room, while Bon had the room upstairs, which was like an attic. He'd painted the room red, and in it he had a little bed and table. I did a Beardsley-inspired drawing for him and he stuck it to the wall. It was the only thing he had that resembled decoration in his room.

Bon was really open and friendly and easy to talk to. I soon discovered that he never judged anyone. He was always up for meeting new people and having a chat.

During the AC/DC days, Bon did an interview with Melbourne journalist Lawrie Masterson, in which he confessed that he'd spent eleven months in jail when he was seventeen. Bon claimed it was for assaulting police. 'I was singing a couple of songs with a band at a dance in Fremantle and a couple of guys started giving me a hard time,' Bon told *The Herald*. 'I got off the stage and got stuck into them. The cops tried to break it up and I finished up on a charge of assaulting the police.'

Bon told me he'd done time in jail, but he refused to elaborate, saying only that he'd broken his mum's heart. It was only when I read Clinton Walker's Bon biography twenty-six years later that I found out what had really happened. At a dance, a sixteen-year-old Bon had sex with an underage girl. A couple of other guys at the dance then tried to force themselves onto the girl and Bon took on both of them. When the police broke up the fight, Bon gave them a false name and address and took off in a mate's car. When he was caught, he ended up in the Fremantle Children's Court, pleading guilty to charges of unlawful carnal knowledge, giving a false name and address to police and having stolen twelve gallons of petrol. He was sent to a boys' home.

Bon was obviously ashamed of what he'd done, and throughout his life he was driven to succeed, partly to say sorry to his mum and dad. From the moment I met Bon, I felt comfortable and completely trusted him. He was the type of guy who respected women.

There would always be plenty of girls at that Dalgety Street house. The guys were starving—if they had some money, they'd wander down to Greasy Joe's for a burger—but there would always be girls at The Valentines' house, cooking and cleaning. And they always had great parties. At one party, I remember Bon running downstairs and grabbing my arm. 'There's a girl in my room,' he whispered. 'Can you get her out of there?'

Bon was concerned that the girl was a little out of it. The next morning, she was sheepish. 'I'm so embarrassed, Mary,' she confided. 'When he got up out of the bed he had one of my false nails stuck on his bum!'

We both laughed.

It was at the Dalgety Street house that I met Gabby. She was a cheeky, pretty young thing, hanging around the band with her friend, Betty. To me, they looked like just young kids. Of course, I was the ripe old age of eighteen!

Around this time, I also encountered Bon's little brother, Graeme. I rocked up to the house one day and knocked on the door. All the boys in the band were asleep—they'd had a gig the night before—and fourteen-year-old Graeme opened the door, and we've been friends ever since. Though he was taller than Bon, you could tell that Graeme was Bon's brother. And Graeme loved his big brother; he worshipped him.

Graeme would have learned a few life lessons at that house. The Valentines started smoking pot after they became friends with an older bloke who lived two doors down. He had a beard and shaggy hair and was always playing cool music. He was a big influence on the guys, introducing them to a band called Rotary Connection, featuring Minnie Riperton on vocals. The music was like a psychedelic trance.

When they had their first smoke, the boys had only a tiny amount of dope, and they wouldn't share any of it with me. They weren't trying to protect me—they just didn't have enough pot to go 'round! Appropriately, the Rotary Connection song I most remember from that time was called 'Turn Me On'.

Mary hanging out by The Valentines' van.

Three strange, hairy characters

Darce

It was the days of 'one band, one van, one roadie'.

In 1968, a young guy named Michael Browning was running a Melbourne club called Sebastian's. He loved Jimi Hendrix and he had discovered a guy in New Zealand, Reno Tehei, who could do the Hendrix act as well as the man himself—right down to the burning guitar and trashing the stack of Marshall amps.

Reno fronted a band called Compulsion, with bass player Ben Kaika and drummer Paddy Beach. Mike Browning brought the band to Melbourne and became their manager.

Compulsion's first appearance in the music press was an article in *Go-Set* on 13 March 1968, which started: 'Are we about to experience Australasia's answer to the Cream and Hendrix?' Reno was described as 'a Maori prince who will one day inherit the title of king'. I'm not sure about that, but he was definitely the king of the guitar.

My flatmate, Daryl, became Compulsion's roadie, driving them around town for about four months. They did a gig with Billy Thorpe, who had just put together a new version of The Aztecs with Lobby Loyde on guitar. Billy asked Daryl if he'd work for them, so Daryl asked me if I would look after Compulsion if he went with Billy.

I loved music—having grown up listening to Elvis, Roy Orbison and Dion—though I knew nothing about setting up music gear. But I said, 'I'll give it a go,' and suddenly I was a roadie. Only problem was I didn't have my driver's licence. I was eighteen, but I'd never bothered going for it. It didn't worry me too much, though, and I was soon behind the wheel of Compulsion's van.

Go-Set wrote about Compulsion: 'three strange, hairy characters . . . they caught the eye of the press with their uncouth ways, their outlandish personalities and their rudeness towards the people they didn't like'.

If someone hung shit on the band, Reno would jump into the crowd and beat them up. And Reno also quickly put the press offside; unfortunately, they seemed to be more interested in the mayhem surrounding Compulsion than the music, which didn't go down too well with Reno. He gave some strange answers in an interview with *Go-Set*, which ran in their issue of 27 March 1968. The headline was 'Compulsion On The Drug Scene In NZ'.

Go-Set: 'Reno, there have been unfavourable reports regarding drug consumption amongst musicians and teenagers in New Zealand.'

Reno: 'Well, man, you can't believe everything you hear. Actually, it is not my scene or business and, for that matter, it is none of your business either.'

Go-Set: 'You seem to misunderstand my question. I'm not suggesting that you take drugs, I'm enquiring about the drug scene in general.'

Reno: 'Well, man, if you really want to know, why don't you just get yourself high and fly LSD to New Zealand? No one would really know the difference. You see, man, most of the junkies are mistaken for drunks. The police aren't quite familiar enough with the effects to be able to tell the difference.'

Go-Set: 'You seem to know the difference.'

Reno: 'Don't get too personal, man. What are you writing about—me or the scene in New Zealand? People took drugs at the club we were playing at, but Mother told me it was bad, so I played it cool and took Aspros. I heard of a cat back home who got high smoking tobacco through a hookah using aftershave lotion with water. But like I said, it is not really my scene, so why ask me, do I look like a junkie?'

Reno certainly wasn't a junkie, but I can tell you that Aspros weren't his only drug of choice. Reno literally turned me on—in a dope sense. He was a big smoker, but I was always reluctant to light up. Then one night I agreed to have a joint. I was driving my flatmate Daryl's Holden ute because he was on the road with Thorpie. I remember that it was raining. The lights were bright and the rain was glistening. The joint accentuated everything. I must have enjoyed it because I soon had another one.

One day, the cops came calling at the Compulsion house.

'We're looking for Reno Tehei,' one cop said.

'That's me,' Reno replied.

'We have reason to believe there are drugs on the premises.'

'No drugs here,' Reno said, as he stubbed out the joint he was smoking.

That was the beauty of Melbourne in 1968—the cops had no idea how to spell marijuana, let alone recognise it.

Mike Browning found the band a house to live in, an old place behind a big church on the corner of Punt Road and Toorak Road in South Yarra. The house was owned by Olivia Newton-John's sister, Rona, and I have to say that the boys didn't really respect the place. They ripped up the floorboards in the hallway for firewood and then covered the hole with a big rug—if you didn't know where to walk, you'd fall to your knees. The guys also didn't bother with crockery. Dinner with Compulsion was not a flash affair. They had drawn circles on the table, where plates would have gone. They would cook up mashed potato and scoop it onto the circles and eat off the table.

Reno and Benny, two Maoris, were wild guys. Whatever Jimi Hendrix did, we did. If we heard that Jimi was dropping acid, we dropped acid. One night, wanting a coffee after a gig, we dropped into Lily's, a restaurant owned by Lily Brett, who was a *Go-Set* writer. I stayed in the van while Reno went to get the coffees. I then heard a commotion, and ran inside to see blokes flying everywhere. Reno had apparently asked someone for a light and he was hit with an ashtray. He then went berserk, trashing the place.

Another night, at the International Club in the city—a popular late-night hangout for bands because you could buy a massive steak for a dollar—Reno got into a brawl with some soldiers. He bit off one guy's ear and threw him down the stairs.

Reno was a tough man, and intimidating. But he was also a loyal friend. If you were a mate, he'd do anything for you. His bandmates loved him. But if he didn't like you . . . look out!

Reno's dislike of journalists only increased over time. 'Reporters Are Nosey Jerks' screamed the headline in *Go-Set*'s issue of 26 June 1968. 'After recent interviews, *Go-Set* reporters have been reluctant to try and get any more information from this angry young man,' started the report, which ran without a byline. 'But due to the many letters requesting a personal interview, we were virtually forced to try again.'

Go-Set: 'Why don't you like reporters?'

Reno: 'Because you're all the same—nosey jerks! And personally I don't need idiots like yourself writing about "how I loved and lost" or that I eat Cornflakes for breakfast. If the kids want to dig me, it's because they dig my music and not because a jerk like you writes a lot of trash about me.'

Fighting with the music press wasn't the smartest idea, though it did get Compulsion plenty of attention. In August 1968, Reno started a feud with *Go-Set*'s leading reporter Molly Meldrum, who was then better known as Ian. The Groove's bass player Jamie Byrne had called Compulsion 'an imitation of Jimi Hendrix' and Molly responded, 'If they sounded like Jimi Hendrix, it wouldn't be too bad . . . I became very bored after seeing them for ten minutes.'

Reno rocked up to the *Go-Set* offices, looking for Molly and Jamie. 'Man, you don't call that constructive criticism,' he thundered to the paper's terrified receptionist. 'It's just a pack of bloody lies.

'Let's face it, Jamie Byrne and his so-called Groove are about as original as the Royal Family . . . and does Jamie Byrne know a good musician when he hears one? I doubt it.'

Reno then found Molly, snapping, 'After talking to *you* for ten minutes, I became a little bored.'

Reno ended the chat: 'Well, baby, you have a habit of dropping names, but have you ever thought what happens in a crowd when somebody drops yours? Best you get back to your fairy tale stories about Johnny Farnham's big blue eyes.'

In *Go-Set*'s first edition for 1969, Molly made his new year's resolutions. For Compulsion, he wished for 'a Jimi Hendrix Australian tour and a polite Reno'.

Reno, however, seemed bulletproof. He could drink 100 per cent proof spirits all day, take a trip and smoke a joint and still do a brilliant gig. Despite his violent side, Reno was a masterful musician. He had been to England, where, the story goes, he turned Eric Clapton on to the wah-wah pedal. Reno had bought the pedal in America, and Clapton was impressed when he saw it in action and offered to buy it from Reno. Another day, Reno borrowed a saxophone from The Twilights, who lived next door. He'd never played the sax before, but that night he played the sax intro to a Traffic song. And he was note perfect! I stood at the side of the stage, shaking my head and wondering, 'How does this crazy guy do it?'

Reno's playing was sophisticated, savage and soulful. As Mike Browning said of Compulsion, 'You do not describe their sound, you *experience* it.' And Paddy was a rocking drummer. He was a tiny guy behind a huge kit, with two bass drums. He was just five foot three and seven-and-a-half stone, but his playing was rock solid. On stage, Compulsion was wild—everyone was on edge, knowing that something crazy could happen at any time. 'They absorb you, tear you to pieces and put you back together again,' Mike told the press. That sounds like a classic piece of hype, but it was actually a fair description.

To get away from being just a Hendrix copy, Compulsion decided to add a lead singer, bringing Issi Dye into the band. I admired Issi's professionalism. Unlike the rest of the band, who would show up to gigs wearing the same gear they'd been in all week, Issi would arrive with several shirts, all on hangers ready to go. Issi stayed for a few months before being replaced by Evan Silva, who had fronted a Kiwi band called The Action. Evan was another wild man, with heaps of energy. He loved to party, but he was a great frontman, with a soulful voice.

Unfortunately, Compulsion never recorded. It was the first band that Mike Browning managed, but it wouldn't be the last.

Evan cleaned up his act and converted to Christianity in 1973. He's now a marriage celebrant in New Zealand and is still making albums. He released an autobiography in 2013 called *Under The Afro*. Reno joined Kevin Borich's La De Das, but unfortunately he got hooked on heroin. He decided to rob his local bank, wearing dark glasses as a 'disguise'. The teller was like, 'Reno, what are you doing?' Not surprisingly, Reno spent some time in jail, before returning to New Zealand.

I still smile when I think about my days with Compulsion. I just wish the band had lasted longer and made a record, something I could play to my kids to show how powerful they were. But Reno and the boys gave me a taste of the rock'n'roll life, and when the band was over, I knew that I wanted more.

Compulsion: Reno, Paddy and Benny.

The motivating metropolis

Darce

Compulsion split in February 1969, with drummer Paddy Beach later hooking up with The Valentines to replace Doug Lavery, who joined Glenn Shorrock and Brian Cadd in Axiom. I didn't really know The Valentines, but I had been to a party at their house in Dalgety Street, St Kilda, when I was working with Compulsion in 1968. It was a crazy night. I remember standing upstairs with Lobby Loyde, surveying the mayhem. 'I thought we were wild,' I remarked, 'but these are crazy fuckers.'

The Valentines had come to Melbourne from Perth. Before The Valentines existed, Bon Scott had been the drummer in The Spektors, one of Perth's top bands, from 1964 to 1966. Vince Lovegrove, the singer in another Perth band, The Winztons, spotted a drummer with 'cute little eyes, pixie-like ears, a turned-up nose and a little Scottish accent'. Bon and The Spektors' guitarist, Wyn Milson, joined forces with The Winztons to form a new band called The Valentines at the end of 1966. Bon didn't want to drum anymore, so he and Vince became The Valentines' co-lead singers. 'We're completely different types,' Vince would later explain. 'We cover each other on stage, making up for each other's deficiencies.'

Still in Fremantle, Bon was working as a postie, while Vince sold pants and shirts at Pellew's Menswear. But they had big rock'n'roll dreams. Their ambition was to move to Melbourne and become the best band in the land.

The Valentines' debut single was a cover of 'Every Day I Have To Cry', written by American country soul singer Arthur Alexander. The song, also known as 'Every Day I Have To Cry Some', had previously been recorded by Dusty Springfield, Ike and Tina Turner, and the Bee Gees. The flipside of The Valentines' single was a cover of the Small Faces' 'I Can't Dance With You'.

The Valentines were immediately supported by Perth radio station 6KY, which was no big surprise because the station's music director, Alan Robertson, had been instrumental in putting the band together, even suggesting the band's name. At the start of 1967, Alan tipped that one Perth group would make it big. 'If it's not the Namelous, it will be the Young Blaydes,' he said. 'If it's not the Young Blaydes, it will be The Valentines. If not them, Mort and the Mokees. Well, you never really know, do you?'

And that last sentence pretty much sums up the entertainment business.

6KY DJ Paul Gadenne contributed the 'West Coast Report' to the Melbourne-based pop paper *Go-Set*. 'My favourite local group, The Valentines, have cut their first single for release through Clarion,' he wrote in the issue of 26 April 1967. 'Although both sides are revivals, I think after listening to the disc you'll like it a whole lot.'

The Clarion label was also home to another Perth singer, Johnny Young.

'Every Day I Have To Cry' hit the WA Top 5, which coincided with the band doing two shows supporting The Easybeats at Perth's His Majesty's Theatre. 'The boys presented this number at the Easybeats shows, much to the glee of their many fans,' Paul Gadenne reported. This was the first time that Bon met George Young, the older brother of Malcolm and Angus. The Easybeats dug The Valentines, and George Young and Harry Vanda wrote a song for the band, 'She Said', which became The Valentines' second single. The B-side was a cover of Phil Spector's 'To Know You Is To Love You' (also known as 'To Know Him Is To Love Him').

The Valentines would end up recording three songs written by Vanda and Young: 'She Said' in 1967, 'Peculiar Hole In The Sky' in 1968 and 'My Old Man's A Groovy Old Man' in 1969.

In July 1967, The Valentines travelled to Melbourne to represent Western Australia in the national final of Hoadley's Battle of the Sounds. This was one of the biggest events in Australian music, a band competition that saw the winners get a trip to London on the Sitmar Line. Sponsored by the confectionery company Hoadley's—the creator of the Violet Crumble bar—the competition ran from 1966 to 1972, with The Twilights the first winners. The second year, 1967, The Groop won, beating Doug Parkinson's band, The Questions, though The Valentines won plenty of fans, with Paul Gadenne reporting in *Go-Set*: 'The Valentines made a good showing of it and did give WA professional representation, as it was thought they would. Since their Melbourne appearance, the boys have received a number of sound offers from "the motivating metropolis".'

Valentines guitarist Ted Junko (who took the stage name Ted Ward) told the Melbourne *Herald* that The Valentines had no plans to head east. 'It's pointless us coming to Melbourne as we are on a good wicket in Perth playing six nights a week,' Ted said.

But Bon and Vince knew they couldn't conquer the world from Perth, and two months later, Paul Gadenne revealed in *Go-Set* that The Valentines were moving to Melbourne. 'Their reasons are mainly due to the fact that the Perth scene is being dominated by the clubs at the moment (The Valentines are not over keen on working for anyone but the teeners) and the fact that to become more specialised in their style of music they need a specialist audience.'

The Valentines—Bon, Vince, Wyn, Ted, bass player John Cooksey and drummer Warwick Findlay—moved to Melbourne in October 1967. The band went with 6KY's blessing, with Paul Gadenne saying, 'The Valentines are willing to start at the bottom and work hard . . . in addition, they're all nice fellows and I wish them the best of luck . . . I don't think we'll see The Valentines back in Perth for a long time because I think they'll make it!'

Paul called Melbourne 'the motivating metropolis', and it was a good time to arrive. King of Pop Normie Rowe had just been called up to serve in Vietnam, so a new pop hero was needed. (Normie didn't dodge the draft, stating in *Go-Set*: 'I don't put myself in a different class to anybody else, so why shouldn't I go and help? I think we've got to fight to keep Communism out of Australia. My ideals are completely anti-Communist.')

The Valentines' arrival also coincided with the start of a new TV music show, *Uptight*, and the opening of a new venue called Bertie's, at number 1 Spring Street in the city. The club took out an ad to promote its launch, with Molly Meldrum stating: 'I can only say that in my vast experience in the disco scene in Melbourne, and indeed the whole world, that unquestionably Bertie's rates absolutely first class.' Max Merritt said, 'It was a pleasant surprise for me to pay sixty-five cents for a meal that would surpass anything from Melbourne's top restaurants.' And Lynne Randell's manager, Carol West, raved: 'I've been to the Daisy in California, Arthur's and Sybilla's in New York, Scott of St James in London—in fact, all of the top places. Bertie's compares favourably with all that I have seen.'

Bertie's was a great club; very modern and upmarket, and we all became regulars. The venue didn't sell alcohol (though Mary was known to smuggle in a little bottle of brandy).

The Valentines' first manager was Gerry Humphreys, who had been the lead singer of The Loved Ones, who split in October 1967 after just one album. The relationship was short-lived, with Vince later claiming, 'He was more out of it than we were.'

It was 1967: the Summer of Love and also a time of psychedelia, LSD, The Beatles, The Monkees and hippies, which Paul Gadenne called '1967's version of the Beatnik and no more intelligent! I have one good thing to say about them—goodbye!'

Go-Set also tipped the demise of the hippie in their 'Trends For 1968' article, written by fashion editor Helen Hopper and 'beauty expert' Molly Meldrum. 'Hippies will be out in

1968,' they declared. 'Whiskers, moustaches and mutton-chop sideboards won't last as a trend much longer. This pop world is one for the young and we think the clean-shaven look will be the image presented in 1968.'

The Valentines received their first record review in *Go-Set* on 21 February 1968, for their third single, 'I Can Hear The Raindrops', which had been written by Vince and Ted. But it wasn't a positive rave. 'Having pledged myself to support Australian talent, it hurts me deeply to be forced into the position of having to review The Valentines' new recording,' Lily Brett wrote. 'I would try to soften the blow, but believe that honesty will basically be more beneficial.'

Lily said the song had 'very pretentious lyrics' and was 'boring, badly recorded, with no imagination shown'.

'I'd advice [*sic*] the Valentines to forget this record very quickly. There, now I've said it! I feel terrible!'

The Valentines did it tough for the first couple of years in Melbourne, stealing food from supermarkets to survive. By the time I started working for the band at the beginning of 1969, they had already released four singles: 'Every Day I Have To Cry', 'She Said', 'I Can Hear The Raindrops' and 'Peculiar Hole In The Sky'.

When they came to record 'Peculiar Hole In The Sky', Warwick Findlay decided to leave the band. He was married and required more security than rock'n'roll could provide. A guy named Doug Lavery wandered into The Bowl, a venue in a basement in Castlereagh Street in Sydney, when The Valentines were rehearsing, and he got talking to Bon.

'What do you play?' Bon asked.

'Drums,' Doug replied.

'Well, okay, we're looking for a drummer.'

'Huh?'

'Warwick's not going to hang around.'

So, Doug—who was playing with Doug Parkinson in Sydney at the time—moved to Melbourne to become The Valentines' new drummer, and the band moved into a house in Dalgety Street, St Kilda. The two-storey joint had room for all the band members—and Bon's pet snake. 'It was a carpet snake, about a metre long,' Doug recalls. 'Bon really loved that snake, but I hated it!' The snake kept escaping from Bon's bedroom, so Doug hid it in a drawer, which did not make Bon happy. Doug wouldn't tell him where the snake was, so they ended up having a fight on the front lawn. Bon chipped Doug's front tooth, but they remained great mates, sharing many bottles of cheap port.

There were plenty of parties at that Dalgety Street house. Girls would often be there in various states of undress; Bon's little brother, Graeme, would stay when he was in town; and Doug woke up one day to find that Barry Humphries had stayed the night.

When The Valentines released 'Peculiar Hole In The Sky', they placed an ad in the music press, pleading, 'Please buy a copy—we're starving.' But the song did not become a hit. The band was building a live vibe, but their records weren't selling.

But, of course, they were paid in different ways. Doug remembers being mobbed by girls at Valentines shows. 'That was hard to take,' he laughs. 'It was like a feeding frenzy.' Molly wrote in *Go-Set* about a Valentines show in Ringwood: 'When Doug, the drummer, got up to sing, he left the stage two minutes later sporting only a pair of red underpants.'

Doug would take over lead vocals for one song, often a cover of 'Yummy Yummy Yummy', while Bon would remember his rock'n'roll roots and return to the seat behind the drum kit.

An on-stage mobbing was a regular occurrence and it became part of the show. If the band wasn't mobbed, it was a bad gig!

Doug drummed with The Valentines for just a few months, before joining 'Australia's first supergroup', Axiom, with Glenn Shorrock, Brian Cadd, Cam-Pact's Chris Stockley and The Groop's Don Mudie. Doug was reluctant to leave The Valentines. 'We weren't a great band, as far as singing and playing went, and we were just doing covers, but we were having fun.' Doug could also see that Bon was an emerging songwriter. 'He was a perfectionist. Every song had to rhyme perfectly.'

Suddenly, The Valentines needed a new drummer—their third in three years. Compulsion had just broken up, so they offered the job to my old mate Paddy Beach.

When I started with the band, Paddy told me they had just released a new single, 'My Old Man's A Groovy Old Man'.

'So's mine,' I replied, 'but what's the record called?'

'That's it.'

'You're having me on!'

After experiencing the club scene with Compulsion, Billy Thorpe and Doug Parkinson, it was strange seeing guys wear candy-coloured outfits, with a fan club made up of girls aged twelve to sixteen. But 'My Old Man's A Groovy Old Man'—which was scheduled for release on Valentine's Day 1969—was a success, becoming the band's first Top 40 hit.

The week after I started as The Valentines' roadie, they were doing a show at Kew Town Hall. This was my test, to see whether I could do the job. The only problem was, the band was yet to break the news to their previous roadie, Mick Christian. They were all too scared to tell him.

Mick was a heavy dude. Fortunately, I knew him—we'd both knocked about on the same streets in our younger years. As a roadie, you've got to be prepared to do just about anything. The Valentines apparently asked Mick to go and buy some guitar strings and he told them to get fucked, he was busy and had his own things to do. Mick wasn't great with the band's young fans either: when they wanted autographs, he would tell them to fuck off.

After their set at Kew Town Hall, Mick was picking up Paddy's drum kit when he spied me at the side of the stage. 'G'day, Darce,' he said. 'What are you doing here?'

'I'm here to do the gig, mate.'

'Is that right?'

'Yeah, mate.'

Mick walked up to the band and snapped, 'You fucking arseholes!' Then he turned around to me and said, 'See you later, mate.' And he took off.

The job was officially mine.

The Valentines in full regalia. Left to right: John Cooksey, Bon, Vince Lovegrove, Ted Junko, Wyn Milson, Doug Lavery. This is one of the last shots to feature Doug in the band.

COCA COLA CO.
PRESENTS
AUSTRALIA'S 1ST
SUPER DANCES
AT BROADMEADOWS
TOWN HALL

Wed. 27th Aug.
AND
Wed. 3rd Sept.
(SCHOOL HOLIDAYS)
8 - 12 P.M.

FEATURING -

★ ★ **DOUG PARKINSON**
IN FOCUS
★ ★ **ZOOT**
★ ★ **FLYING CIRCUS**
★ ★ **HEART and SOUL**
★ ★ BRISBANE **AVENGERS**
★ ★ **TOWN CRIERS**
★ ★ **AXIOM**
★ ★ **JON BLANCHFIELD**
★ ★ **WENDY SADDINGTON**
★ ★ **LEO and the BROWNS**
★ ★ **DAISY CLOVER**
★ ★ **IGUANA**
★ ★ **PLUM**

20c CONCESSION IF PRESENTED
BEFORE 8.30 p.m.

DRINK
Coca-Cola
things go
better
with
Coke

The impressive line-up for a couple of gigs at Broadmeadows Town Hall, 1969.

The Valentines drummer, Doug Lavery, remembers the band's two lead singers, Vince Lovegrove and Bon Scott: 'Vince was very goofy, Bon was more hard-arsed. They were like chalk and cheese on stage, which was great. It wasn't like the Everly Brothers; these guys were so different.'

'Can you swim?'

Gabby

I became a Valentines fan because my friend Betty loved them. She'd say to me, 'There's this group . . . I think you'll like them.'

And that's what you did in the sixties—you followed groups. On my bedroom wall were posters of The Valentines, Zoot and The Masters Apprentices.

Just about every town hall in Melbourne had dances, where bands would play. Michael Gudinski ran a dance at Caulfield Town Hall, which I could walk to. Betty and I would drag along my twelve-year-old brother, Mark. I think he learned a lot from those outings.

The first time I saw The Valentines was at the Myer Music Bowl in March 1969. It was the 3UZ Moomba Pop Show with The Valentines, Zoot, Ronnie Burns, Johnny Farnham, The Masters Apprentices, Johnny Chester, The Groop and Russell Morris. It was war between the Zoot and Valentines' fans. The Zoot fans were prissy; we were hardcore.

'The Valentines and the Zoot fought out their popularity war,' *Go-Set* reported. 'Both had tons of fans—the Valentines dressed in blue, the Zoot naturally in pink.' To help them stand out from the crowd, Zoot's manager, Wayne de Gruchy, decided that all the band members would dress in pink, which was an outrageous look for men in the sixties. Their promotional campaign was 'Think Pink—Think Zoot'. The band—Darryl Cotton, Beeb Birtles, Roger Hicks and Rick Brewer—dressed in head-to-toe pink satin. Darryl had a pink car, and they even painted Darryl's dog, Monty, pink for a photo shoot. There's a great saying in the music business: 'If it's worth doing, it's worth overdoing.'

More than 150,000 people turned up for the five-hour show at the Myer Music Bowl, and we were right down the front. Bands and artists had tribal followings back in those days. The Bowl show hit the headlines because the crowd started booing Johnny Farnham during his second song. Molly blasted the fans, calling them 'rude and ignorant' and reported that Johnny was 'close to tears'. But that was the nature of the pop business back then—you could have only one favourite, and every other act was the enemy.

After the show, we went around to the back of the Bowl to meet the band. Mickey Christian was The Valentines' roadie. Everyone was scared of Mickey—everyone except for us. We taunted him, so he chased us with a hammer, threatening to kill us. We were cheeky; Mickey was a madman.

It was an exciting time to be a teenager. Stan Rofe was Melbourne's leading radio DJ in the sixties—everyone listened to 'Stan the Man'. He also wrote a column in *Go-Set* called 'Stan Rofe's Tonic'. 'The Zoot and The Valentines led the return back to teenage rock and now it seems nearly every other group wants to join the invasion,' Stan wrote in *Go-Set* on 3 May 1969. 'Looks like the kids are in for a feast, and about time, I say.'

We all religiously read *Go-Set*. It was our bible. Mary was even the paper's first winner of their fashion-design competition. She drew the coolest outfit—flares, a puffy-sleeved shirt and a bolero—and winning first prize meant she got to go to the *Go-Set* office and pick any album she wanted (she chose a Dionne Warwick record). Betty and I were very envious—Mary was older than us, cooler and more sophisticated, *and* she'd been to the *Go-Set* office.

The *Go-Set* issue of 12 March 1969 featured an article by Molly Meldrum, entitled 'Valentines Suffer Acute Case Of Screaming And Hysteria'.

He declared that a new generation of teenagers and pop bands had revitalised the scene, 'and the long lost excitement finally returned'.

'The first group to cause teenage hysteria wherever they appeared was the Zoot. Now, following right on their heels are the cupids of the Australian pop business, The Valentines.'

'The whole scene has really kicked on,' Vince told Molly. 'In Melbourne, the day of the screamers has returned.'

Molly said the turning point for The Valentines was their Valentine's Day gig at That's Life, a club on Chapel Street in Prahran. And Betty and I were there. It was an incredible bill: The Valentines, Johnny Farnham, Daisy Clover, Max Merritt & The Meteors and The Masters Apprentices. And The Valentines stole the show, with the crowd chanting, '*We love The Valentines!*' I'll never forget that show; Betty and I were hoarse at the end of it. Bon and Vince threw cupids into the audience—I still have one of them—and the crowd responded by throwing bubblegum and then storming the stage, dragging Bon to the ground and ripping off his pants and jacket.

Bon loved it.

Betty was the leader of our little duo. I was always a couple of steps behind. Betty was gorgeous, with shiny blonde hair, long legs and a beautiful face. Betty was the one. She had everything.

And she was madly in love with Vince.

It took Vince a long time to take us seriously, but in his own way, I think he was also in love with Betty. They ended up having a brief romantic entanglement, but in the crazy rock'n'roll world, the relationship was never going to endure.

Bon and Paddy Beach were my favourite Valentines. I thought they were spunks. I would cut their photos out of magazines and stick them on my schoolbooks. Vince was off-limits, because Betty liked him. Not that I found Vince attractive. Vince and Bon shared the singing duties in The Valentines, but Vince got most of the press, because he was the official spokesman for the band. And the press seemed to love him because he was intelligent and quotable.

'We're Better Than The Zoot!' screamed the headline in *Go-Set* in June 1969.

The article, by Lindy Hobbs (who later lived with Al Pacino), started: 'He has a lot to say and what's more he knows how to say it.'

Vince let fly at The Valentines' arch rivals: 'Frankly, I'll be surprised if the Zoot last more than six months. They have only survived this long due to constant publicity, good promotion and teenybopper-appeal gimmicks. We've always considered ourselves far better musically.'

Vince then tried to claim that the feud was all Zoot's fault. 'To tell the truth, Zoot's attitude towards us is quite ridiculous. They seem to think there's some big feud, which is probably a cover-up for jealousy because when they arrived from Adelaide, we tried to be hospitable, taking them out to dinner and so forth. Now, they don't even know us. Anyway, we don't regard them as competition.'

Vince also took a shot at *Go-Set*'s star reporter, saying, 'Even God shouldn't be entitled to the influence Ian Meldrum has over the pop scene.' And he declared that The Masters Apprentices' singer, Jim Keays, had 'the worst voice I have ever heard'.

Lindy asked Vince about his relationship with Bon and whether he was happy sharing the limelight. 'Yes,' he replied, 'I think The Valentines are where they are today because of our unique two-singer combination. The audiences don't get sick of us, while there is no cause for either of us to be overworked.'

Lindy: 'You're avoiding my question—would you prefer to be the solo lead singer?'

Vince: 'Oh, no, definitely not. Admittedly, I'm more popular than Bon, but he's a far better singer than I'll ever be. In fact, I think he's the most underrated singer in Australia.'

Lindy's article had a sting in its tail: 'So, there you have it—Vince Lovegrove's candid comments. Even if he can't sing, he sure can talk.'

That article caused quite a stir, and the following week Vince backtracked in the pages of *Go-Set*: 'I did NOT say I was more popular than Bon. I simply said he is a far better singer than I am.

'I did NOT mean that we're better than the Zoot. I simply said that we feel we are more experienced and better musically than the Zoot.

'And I didn't say that Jim Keays had "the worst voice I'd ever heard". I said that I think his voice is almost as bad as mine.'

There's no doubt that Vince's outlandish statements caused plenty of grief for The Valentines, but civil war was averted because Bon was such a friendly, outgoing guy. He befriended just about everyone he met, so other bands simply couldn't bring themselves to hate The Valentines, even if they were offended by Vince's comments.

But let me tell you, the pop rivalry was real. Zoot drummer, Rick Brewer, accused The Valentines of jumping on their bandwagon after the Zoot's 'Think Pink' campaign. 'I think The Valentines are kidding themselves a bit because they depend on overseas records to get by in preference to originality,' Rick sniped in *Go-Set*. 'I think they should try to be themselves.'

Fans, radio DJs and rock writers were forced to choose sides. Molly denied that he supported the Zoot ahead of The Valentines, though Bon hit back: 'What a hypocrite, Ian—you are still wearing pink!'

Every year, *Go-Set* ran a 'Pop Poll', inviting its readers to vote for their favourite acts. In 1969, Betty and I voted for The Valentines, of course, and we expected them to battle it out with the Zoot for the title of Best Australian Group. We were devastated when we got the paper at the end of June and were confronted by the headline: 'Zoot Beats Masters In Recount!'

The paper received more than 20,000 votes, and Zoot beat The Masters Apprentices by forty-five votes. The expected showdown between the Zoot and The Valentines didn't eventuate, with the Top 10 showing The Valentines coming in at a disappointing number nine:

1. Zoot
2. The Masters Apprentices
3. The Brisbane Avengers
4. The Dream
5. The Flying Circus
6. The Town Criers
7. The Dave Miller Set
8. Doug Parkinson in Focus
9. The Valentines
10. The Groove

We were devastated. And the *Go-Set* writers were surprised. 'I am staggered this group did not poll better,' Molly wrote. 'The Valentines are one of the best stage acts in Australia. Their singles are first-class, but what they need is overall national exposure.' Stan Rofe agreed, saying they're 'not truly a national name as yet—most of their votes came from Melbourne'. While David Elfick, who ran *Go-Set*'s Sydney office, tipped they 'should poll better next year'.

The Pop Poll result merely stiffened our resolve—Betty and I remained committed to The Valentines. We'd hitchhike or catch the train to their gigs; whatever it took. We'd go to two gigs a night, sometimes three—it all depended on how much we lied to our mums and whether we had to go home. We had Saturday morning jobs—I worked at a pharmacy—so we were always flush with money.

The night would often start with a gig at the Paradise in Ormond. If we were babysitting Betty's little brother, ten-year-old John, and twelve-year-old sister, Judy (who would appear in Bon's life a few years later), we'd take them to the Moorabbin Bowl and leave them there.

The band's second gig for the night would often be at the Frankston Mechanics Hall, so we'd jump on the train and head to Frankston. Then we'd return to the ten-pin bowling alley and pick up the kids. If we weren't babysitting, we'd hitchhike into the city to see The Valentines' late show at Bertie's or Sebastian's, which would go until two or three in the morning.

Even though we were underage, we got to know the bouncers, and they'd always let us in. We'd then huddle at the front and wait for the band to hit the stage. The Valentines always put on a big show. Often, the gig would start with a multi-coloured smoke bomb. When the smoke cleared, the crowd would see Vince and Bon perched on top of the amps, waving sparklers. It sounds primitive by today's standards, but in 1969 this was an impressive stage show. 'It brings the crowd to fever pitch,' Molly wrote in *Go-Set*.

Molly reported that the only hitch with the show was a clothing problem. 'Because of their current wave of popularity, The Valentines' biggest problem is their stage outfits. Instead of sticking to one particular colour in costumes, The Valentines prefer to have three or four different coloured outfits to add variety. Unfortunately it is very costly as Vince and Bon have at least three shirts torn off their backs every week.

'Subsequently,' Molly joked, 'the boys are seriously thinking of outfitting themselves in tin armour.'

There was definitely a sexual side to The Valentines' show. Michele O'Driscoll, who wrote under the name Mitch, stated in *Go-Set*: 'Often the suggestive nature of Vince Lovegrove's stage movements could be called "indecent", but there are few complaints from the worshipping fans.'

Vince explained in an interview with *Go-Set* that the band didn't want to project a 'queer' image. 'For too long now groups and artists have been preoccupied with promoting a "camp" image for the sake of managers and promoters—they seem to have forgotten that the raw sex appeal of the artist radiated to the girls in the audience was the biggest part of Presley, Tom Jones, Normie Rowe, The Beatles, the Stones, The Doors and lots of others.'

In 1969, The Valentines had a second shot at glory in Hoadley's Battle of the Sounds, in which they had made the national final two years earlier. 'Unlike previous years, there appears to be no definite favourite to win the coveted prize,' Molly wrote in his Battle of the Sounds preview, adding that The Valentines' 'stage act alone is enough to place them in the top three'.

The Valentines' odds shortened when Zoot were surprisingly knocked out of the competition in their Melbourne heat, beaten by a band called Nova Express, featuring Linda George on vocals. At the final, at Melbourne's Festival Hall, The Valentines performed a medley of 'Nick Nack Paddy Wack', 'Getting Better' and 'My Old Man's A Groovy Old Man'. They were great, we screamed, and . . . they came third, behind Doug Parkinson in Focus and Aesop's Fables. It was another blow for the band, though *Go-Set*'s Stan Rofe urged them to try again, saying, 'My nomination for the 1970 Battle (providing they stick together) is The Valentines by a mile.'

We weren't the only girls chasing The Valentines all over town. Three other girls—whom we called the Jumbo Twins and Little Kerry—were also at just about every gig. It was a strange sight: red-headed Kerry was about four foot tall and heavily pregnant. (We never found out who the father was.) And the Jumbo Twins were big blonde girls. They were tough chicks from the other side of town, and we had only one thing in common—our love of The Valentines. And that was enough for the Jumbo Twins. Things could get a little heated between the Zoot and Valentines' fans, but we knew it would never get physical because none of the Zoot fans would dare take on the Twins.

Betty and I would regularly visit The Valentines at their Toorak Road flat. We would often bump into Johnny Farnham in the stairwell, but he was off-limits because his manager, Darryl Sambell, was very protective. We'd also see Johnny Young, but he had a different type of fan. They seemed like 'sweet' girls, not wild and crazy, like The Valentines' fans, and they didn't hang around waiting for him in the stairwell.

I met Darcy at the flat. I thought he was cute, but it wasn't an instant attraction. I got to know him better when Betty and I went on The Valentines' fan club picnic. The band hired a bus and took their fans to the Belgrave Pool, which was a major day trip back in those days.

Bon's younger brother, Graeme, was in town, so he also came along. Graeme is two years older than me, and we enjoyed hanging out together. He was a merchant seaman and he'd always catch up with the band whenever he was in Melbourne. He really idolised his brother, and Bon loved having him around.

When I boarded the bus, I found that all the boys were down the back and there was no room for me. I had to take a seat near the front of the bus. But then Darcy came to sit next to me. I remember he took the window seat and we talked all the way up to Belgrave.

At the pool, another one of The Valentines' female fans, Marcelle, was saying how cute she thought Darcy was. 'He's so gorgeous,' she cooed.

'Can you swim?' I asked her.

'No.'

'Good,' I said. And I pushed her in the pool.

That's when I realised that I liked Darcy.

There was another girl who used to hang out with Darce and Paddy in South Yarra. I think I pushed her off a tram.

I *really* liked Darce.

Darcy had to ask the boys in the band if it was okay for him to go out with me; I think he was worried that I was too young. Darce was twenty-one, but I was sixteen, and my Mum approved.

Darcy asked me if I would go out with him. And I said yes.

Bon and Darce having a cuddle just outside the Belgrave Pool.

Beeb Birtles, Zoot bass player: 'Zoot were the first band to dress alike in uniforms and many of the other Melbourne bands followed suit. Of course, The Valentines didn't have anywhere near the same success with their recordings as we did. I think the rivalry existed from the time Zoot moved to Melbourne from Adelaide. What can I say, we were just a better looking group!

'When we were looking for a new lead guitarist the rivalry really escalated. Zoot, The Valentines and the Brisbane Avengers were all courting Rick Springfield for his services. Roger Hicks left Zoot and joined the Brisbane Avengers, and Rick Springfield thought it would benefit him more to join Zoot.

'The Valentines were dirty boys compared to Zoot. Zoot was innocent and pretty pure compared to other bands. My most vivid memory of Bon is that he always had a smile on his face and he was always very friendly towards me. I loved watching him on stage, the way he would stand with his legs bowed out and giving it all he had vocally.'

Blowing bubbles

Gabby

When you're a teenager, your favourite band can do no wrong. Betty and I absolutely adored The Valentines. Every gig was special and we played every single until we wore out the grooves.

In August 1968, The Valentines released their fourth single. The A-side was the second song that Vanda and Young gave the band, a song called 'Peculiar Hole In The Sky', while the flipside was The Valentines' cover of Soft Machine's 'Love Makes Sweet Music', which DJ Stan Rofe suggested to the band.

'Peculiar Hole In The Sky' copped some bad reviews at the time—'It was probably only recorded because it was penned by The Easybeats,' *Go-Set* reckoned—but to my ears, it's a sweet slice of psychedelic pop. If The Monkees had recorded it, it would have been a smash hit.

The Valentines recorded the single in Sydney with Pat Aulton, who had produced all of Normie Rowe's hits and would later co-write and produce 'It's Time', the Labor Party campaign song that would help Gough Whitlam get elected in 1972.

By the time 'Peculiar Hole In The Sky' was released, The Valentines had been in Melbourne for nearly a year and they were still chasing that elusive hit. Molly Meldrum wrote about the band in *Go-Set* in August 1968 in a piece headed 'Valentines Are Raring To Go', stating that when they arrived in Melbourne and released the Vanda-and-Young-penned 'She Said', the band 'sat back and thought they would make hay while the sun shines. Unfortunately, the sun has been hidden by a cloud to this day'.

Molly mentioned that the band had been plagued by management dramas, though Vince admitted, 'The fault was not only the manager's, it was partly our fault, too. The whole lot of us had been lazy and weren't prepared to help ourselves.'

Molly called the single 'a sure-shot hit'. 'At last, the weather has broken for The Valentines; clear, sunny days are ahead.

'As much as my name is Hedda Hepper,' Molly added, pretending to be the newspaper columnist from *The Lucy–Desi Comedy Hour*, 'the Valentines are sure to make a lot of hay in the next six months.' I wasn't exactly sure what Molly was on about, but I think he was saying that The Valentines were going to be big, which made us very happy.

Each week, Betty and I would grab a copy of *Go-Set*, turn to page 2 and scan the charts, to see if The Valentines had made it. We were giddy with excitement when we found that 'Peculiar Hole In The Sky' had entered the Australian Top 15 at number eleven on 28 August 1968. It was a long way from number one (Johnny Farnham's 'I Don't Want To Love You'/'Jamie'), and it wasn't *Go-Set*'s main chart, but it was a start. Surely the song would rocket to the top the following week?

But when we bought the next issue of *Go-Set*, we discovered that the single had slipped to number thirteen. *This must be a mistake,* we thought. Things improved a little the following week, with the single rising to number twelve. And then it dropped out of the charts altogether.

What was going on?

Betty was then beside herself when she read Molly's story about The Valentines touring Brisbane and raving about the pop scene up there. 'We love Melbourne and we want to stay here,' Vince said. 'But believe me, Melbourne has a lot to learn from Brisbane about a Top 40 scene.' The Valentines wouldn't desert us and move to Brisbane, would they? We needed to be more devoted than ever.

To attract attention, many pop bands in the sixties decided they needed an image. Zoot, for example, had their 'Think Pink—Think Zoot' campaign. Of course, the problem with any image is that it inevitably leads to a backlash. Many people referred to Zoot as 'pink pansies'. Whenever they had a chart success, the pop writers said the band was 'tickled pink'. By the start of 1970, the Zoot were sick of the pink image and held a ceremonial burning of their pink outfits live on TV, on *Happening '70*. And when Rick Springfield joined the band, they released a single called 'Hey Pinky', which was a shot at everyone who had bagged them for wearing pink.

To stand out from the crowd, The Valentines declared that they were a bubblegum group. American record producers Jerry Kasenetz and Jeff Katz, who worked with bands such as The Ohio Express and 1910 Fruitgum Company, claim credit for coming up with the term. The story goes that when they were trying to work out the target market for their music they were chewing bubblegum. 'Ah, this is like bubblegum music,' they exclaimed.

Bubblegum songs were very catchy and often cheesy, with titles such as 'Yummy Yummy Yummy' and 'Sugar, Sugar'.

Vince made The Valentines' New Year's resolution in *Go-Set*'s first issue for 1969: 'To answer my mail more promptly and try to make Valentines fans eat more bubblegum.' Molly Meldrum's wishes for the band were 'a year's supply of bubblegum, a fairy floss machine, a sweet little hit and a new image'.

Go-Set included The Valentines in its article on 'Groups Most Likely To Succeed In 69', but it wasn't a glowing endorsement: 'The Valentines' stars are a little hazy,' the paper stated. 'Everything points to success, but their biggest hang-up will be that bubblegum music will be old-hat by March. The Valentines will then have to take stock of themselves and aim for a sound that is completely original. They will always be one of Australia's most popular groups, but like many before them, the number one crown will evade their grasp.'

Bigger things were tipped for our arch rivals. 'The Zoot will be the rave for '69. They will be the biggest thing to happen to the Australian pop scene since The Easybeats.'

Once The Valentines declared they were a bubblegum band, bubblegum was mentioned in just about every article about them. It was both a curse and a blessing. 'For a change, The Valentines over Christmas chewed on plum pudding in preference to bubblegum,' Molly wrote in his *Go-Set* column at the start of 1969. 'Seen around town eating bubblegum,

The Valentines continue to blow hard,' Stan Rofe added in his column.

After an interview with the band, Molly finished his article by saying, 'The Valentines then left the *Go-Set* offices to buy some sweet lollies at the corner milk bar.'

Doug Lavery explained the band's approach: 'In our opinion, bubblegum music is just a name which has been adopted in America and Australia for commercial-type happy Top 40 music. We are basically a teenage group trying to appeal to young teenagers and so we decided that we would adopt the term "bubblegum group".'

Bass player John Cooksey said The Valentines were trying to project 'a very happy, sweet, but sexy commercial-type image'.

Bon spoke about the band's new single, 'My Old Man's A Groovy Old Man'/'Ebeneezer', saying that 'both sides are bouncy, happy, lollipop songs. Very commercial.'

The Twilights broke up at the start of 1969 and their parting words included a wish for The Valentines: 'A year's supply of bubblegum, to help their group stick together.'

The serious music critics didn't really rate bands such as The Valentines and Zoot. 'Soul groups' had the credibility; the bubblegum bands had the screaming fans, like Betty and me. The cover of *Go-Set*'s issue of 2 April 1969 put the two genres head to head: Soul groups (Max Merritt, Billy Thorpe and Wendy Saddington) versus Bubblegum (The Valentines, Zoot and The Avengers).

Max Merritt said he didn't like bubblegum music (The Valentines responded by calling Max 'overrated'). Wendy Saddington agreed with Max, saying that she thought the kids would soon tire of the chewy stuff and 'come around to her kind of music'. But Billy Thorpe said: 'We think it [bubblegum] is very good and we have nothing at all against it. It's very easy for kids to dance to. It's very simple music, really. We wouldn't play it ourselves, but we do like it.'

I agreed with Thorpie. There was nothing wrong with bubblegum pop. You had to be a musical snob of the highest order not to like it. And as Paddy Beach said when he became the new drummer in The Valentines, replacing Doug Lavery: 'Let's face it, most underground groups play a lot of rubbish.'

We could sense that things were improving for The Valentines in 1969. The crowds at their gigs were getting bigger, and the screaming was getting louder. 'My Old Man's A Groovy Old Man' made its first appearance on *Go-Set*'s Australian Top 15 on 24 May, at number fourteen (Russell Morris's 'The Real Thing' was at number one) and leapt into the Top 10 the following week. It looked like The Valentines were going to score their first national hit. And it happened on 5 July, with the single entering *Go-Set*'s National Top 40 at number thirty-seven.

Betty and I tracked the song's progress. It moved up three spots, to thirty-four, the following week. Then it jumped to number twenty-eight, and *Go-Set* showed that it was the fifth-biggest home-grown hit in the country. But it was only charting in Victoria and Queensland . . . what were the other states doing?!

'My Old Man's A Groovy Old Man' jumped from 27 to 23 on 2 August, and that was it—the song had peaked. But the band had already released another single in Melbourne, 'Nick Nack Paddy Wack', which built on the old nursery rhyme. Vince called it 'very catchy and sing-alongish'. *Go-Set*'s record reviewer, Ed Nimmervoll, wasn't so sure, arguing, 'I think we could have well done without the "Nick Nack Paddy Wack" lyric . . . but the group does insist on classifying themselves as "bubblegum", so I guess it's as valid as "Yummy Yummy" and "Chewy Chewy".'

But Molly Meldrum dug it, writing, 'I love, yes LOVE, the Valentines' new single . . . it's a beauty.' He also praised the B-side, 'Getting Better', which Bon wrote with Wyn. 'It wouldn't surprise me if this side doesn't become the big hit. The Valentines have certainly shot to the forefront over the last two months.'

This is it, Betty and I thought. *The Valentines are going to be superstars.*

Go-Set: the Bible. Gab catching up on all the gossip.

On the night that Robert Kennedy was killed, on 5 June 1968, Mike Brady sold life insurance to Bon Scott.

Mike had been a member of sixties band MPD Ltd with Danny Finley and Pete Watson. They had a number one hit in Melbourne in 1965 with their version of 'Little Boy Sad'.

To supplement his music income, Mike got a job selling insurance for T&G Insurance. 'I "preyed" on my contacts,' Mike says. As well as Bon, Mike sold life insurance to Vince Lovegrove, Phil Manning, Jim Keays and Rick Springfield.

Mike would later write the classic footy anthem 'Up There Cazaly'.

Be my Valentine

Mary

During The Valentines days, Bon had one major love: an American girl named Michelle.

Doug Lavery, the band's drummer before Paddy Beach, met a girl named Pauline at The Thumpin' Tum, one of Melbourne's major rock clubs in the sixties. They fell in love and decided to get married. Bon fell for Pauline's sister, Michelle, and a double wedding was planned. But then the girls' father, Sonny, arrived. Michelle's dad liked Doug but took an instant dislike to Bon. The double wedding was off.

If truth be told, I actually fancied Doug. But when I found out he had a girlfriend, I backed off. And when I met Pauline, we became great friends. Her mum was a little suspicious of my motives—'Are you crazy?' she told Pauline. 'This girl is going to steal your boyfriend!' But Pauline knew that I was not that kind of girl.

I was a bridesmaid for Doug and Pauline's wedding. Vince was the best man, and Bon was an usher; it was the only time we ever saw Bon in a suit. It was a lovely day. One image on the dance floor remains embedded in my mind: when the music stopped, Bon and Michelle kept spinning, completely absorbed in each other. The look on Sonny's face was one of blind fury. I knew then that the relationship was doomed.

Michelle's parents had divorced, and while Michelle and her father lived in America, her mother, Violet, moved to Australia with the two youngest daughters, Pauline and Valerie. They lived at the housing commission flats in Carlton, and the band often went to the flat for dinner. Michelle's mum loved Bon and the boys, and was always happy to cook up a big bowl of spaghetti bolognaise. The only weird night was when Violet went out and we scored some pot. We forced Val to go to bed, while Michelle, Pauline and I got ridiculously stoned. We were lying on the floor, hallucinating and laughing hysterically. Violet could smell the dope when she got home and she yelled at Michelle and Pauline, but we denied everything. The pot was so much nicer in those days; it was real giggly stuff. Then it became over-manufactured, which just resulted in me getting paranoid, and I just stopped. I haven't smoked pot since 1975.

Michelle, in her early twenties, came to Australia to visit her mum and sisters, and also because she was dealing with a break-up. She never expected to fall in love in Melbourne. After she met the band through Pauline, Vince pursued her initially, but she wasn't interested. Then she and Bon fell in love.

There was an interesting rivalry between Vince and Bon. I guess having two lead singers would always lead to some tension, but I think it was more on Vince's side—Bon didn't seem to care. They were a little like brothers, competing to see who would get the girl.

Michelle gave up her job in America to stay in Australia with Bon, hoping that her father would come to approve of the relationship.

One of the first songs Bon ever wrote was about Michelle. It was called 'Getting Better' and it was the B-side of The Valentines' 1969 single, 'Nick Nack Paddy Wack'. It spoke of his devastation when she decided to leave, and then how overjoyed he was when she reconsidered and decided to stay.

The sisters used to call me 007. When The Valentines were doing a gig, the girls would stay at home and play cards with their mother for money. 'We're not interested in going to the gig,' Michelle told me. 'You're 007, you make sure the guys behave themselves.'

So, I'd keep an eye on the boys.

Around this time, I was going out with The Valentines' guitarist, Wyn. It kind of happened accidentally; we were just hanging out and then suddenly we were going out. He was a lovely, easy-going guy, but it was no big romance. In some ways, I had more in common with the band's other guitarist, Ted. He was also Ukrainian, though he changed his surname from Junko to Ward.

My Mum loved having the boys over for dinner. She treated Doug and Pauline to a traditional Ukrainian meal, starting with borshch (a beetroot soup), followed by varenyky (a soft dumpling filled with mashed potato and bacon) and holubtsi (cabbage rolls filled with meat and rice).

When Vince came over, my Dad tried to ply him with homemade vodka, but it was too much for him, and I had to drink Vince's share when my Dad wasn't looking.

When Bon found out that the other band members had had dinner with my Mum and Dad, he confronted me. 'All the others get to meet your parents,' he complained. 'Except me.'

I thought he was joking, so I laughed. But then I realised that he was genuinely upset. I regret not asking him to my family home; I don't know why I didn't invite him. My mother would have loved him—every mother loved Bon.

There was a spiritual side to Bon: I remember he told me that one morning during The Valentines days, he woke up to find a ghost sitting at the end of his bed. On another occasion, as The Valentines headed to Geelong for a gig, Bon didn't travel with them—he stayed behind to visit Michelle's mum's best friend, Sylvia, a fortune teller. Sylvia told Bon that he would marry a blonde and a redhead. I always thought this was a little strange because he would go on to marry Irene, who was blonde, and later give his wedding ring to me, a redhead.

Sylvia also predicted that Bon would end up in a band in which he would play 'a weird instrument'. Do the bagpipes qualify as a weird instrument?

The fortune teller also told Bon that he would die young, which freaked him out. He ended up running late for the Geelong gig, though he managed to get a lift there and arrived just before the band was due on stage.

Darcy refused to visit Sylvia, saying he didn't want to be freaked out. 'Whatever happens, will happen,' he said. 'And I'll just let it happen.' Not a bad philosophy, really.

Michelle's father, Sonny, didn't mind Pauline marrying Doug. But of course he hated Bon, and he wasn't happy that his youngest daughter, Val, who was only fourteen or fifteen, had a mad crush on Vince. When Michelle told her father that she loved Bon, he slapped her face and ordered: 'You're coming home with me!'

Michelle told me she didn't want to disobey her father and she was worried about what he might do to Bon. Her dad owned a nightclub in Houston. 'He's very well connected,' Michelle said. 'He knows people. You wouldn't want to mess with him.'

So, Michelle returned to America—without Bon. He was so wounded, he didn't go to the airport to say goodbye.

Years later, when AC/DC played in Houston, Bon tracked down Michelle's phone number and called her after the show. She whispered into the phone because she didn't want to wake her husband. Bon was reminiscing, reliving their intimate moments, explaining how much he regretted the end of their relationship.

'Will you come and see me?' Bon pleaded.

'Bon, I can't,' Michelle said. 'I've just had a baby.'

Again, the timing wasn't right. Michelle had just come home from hospital after giving birth. She hung up the phone and started crying. Some things just aren't meant to be.

The happy couples:
Bon and Michelle, Doug and Pauline at the girls' mum's flat in Carlton.

Wyn and Mary.

Suited and booted on the corner of Punt Road and Toorak Road, at Pauline and Doug Lavery's wedding. Left to right: John Cooksey, Wyn, Ted and Bon.

Mary: 'This is the first and last time I ever saw Bon in a suit.'

During The Valentines days, Bon was profiled in a pop paper:

Likes: My room (painted red), long blonde hair, sex, showers, swimming.

Dislikes: People who hate Crater Critters [Crater Critters were little plastic toys inserted in Kellogg's Corn Flakes in 1968], *being disturbed whilst thinking, washing and ironing.*

Loves: Parents, my pet Crater Critter.

Favourite food: Ice cream.

Drink: Sand Zombie.

Actor: Vince.

Actress: Julie Christie, Vanessa Redgrave.

Groups: Beatles, Moody Blues.

Singer, Male: John Lee Hooker, Otis Redding.

Singer, Female: The Supremes.

Transporting seafood

Darce

Roadies aren't conventional people—we are never going to work nine to five. Rock'n'roll is a great job: there is no one telling you what to wear or to cut your hair.

That's not to say I didn't work hard during The Valentines years. I had to drive the band to all their gigs, set up their gear and then pack up and load the gear back into the van, and drive to the next gig. If any equipment needed maintenance, I did that; I got amplifiers fixed, bought strings and drumsticks. And I'd get up in the morning and buy the milk and papers. In short, I made sure that everything kept flowing.

When the band was on stage, I was setting microphone levels and keeping an eye on the gear. I had to be ready in case a lead failed or a cymbal was knocked over. Things got a little crazy during the gigs when screaming girls invaded the stage. I also looked after the band's PA. Most bands in the sixties would hire a PA, but Bon got Lobby Loyde to design and build our system. It was as tall as me, with a 1000-watt head. It weighed a ton, but it was pretty flash for the time!

For my work, I was paid $100 cash a week, which was good money in 1969, especially when I was cruising around in ripped jeans and T-shirt, working with a band and dealing with a lot of young chicks.

Vince was in charge of the money. Every week, he would visit the band's manager, Bill Joseph, to do the dollars, then return to our flat and hand out the envelopes. Vince short-changed me numerous times. I'd open my envelope and it would contain only ninety bucks. 'What happened, Vince?'

'No worries, mate,' he'd say. 'I'll make it up next week when I go to the office.'

The following week, I'd get my usual $100—I'd still be $10 short.

If Vince did it to me, he did it to everyone. He ended up not doing the dollars; he couldn't help himself, he was just that sort of person, always looking for perks—and to get into some girl's pants. He didn't hang much with the band; scoring chicks seemed to be Vince's top priority. We'd be at the flat, waiting for Vince to arrive with our money—so we could go out and get some food—and Vince would always be 'sidetracked'. And he'd always return with some sort of trophy. 'Look, I got these boots!' he'd say. Or, 'I scored this cool leather belt.' It was like a sexual souvenir.

I'll never forget the day at the flat when Vince came out of the shower, and addressed the rest of the band. 'I can't fuck anymore,' he declared.

'What?' I said. I thought it was some sort of joke, but Vince had a serious look on his face.

'I just can't fuck anymore—all the skin's come off me knob.'

That's how frequently the girls threw themselves at us.

When I'd go to the shop every morning to buy the milk and newspapers, there would be four or five girls sitting outside our flat, at the top of the stairs. 'Are the guys up?'

'No, they're still asleep.'

'Can we get some autographs?'

'Yeah, we'll get some later.'

After about half-an-hour up the street, I'd return to discover about a dozen girls outside the flat. By 11 a.m., it would be more like twenty; they'd be lined up down the stairs.

'Can we see the boys?' they'd ask.

'Yeah, they'll be out later.'

By 4 p.m., the sixteen-year-olds would start turning up, all made up, in their mini-skirts.

'Come on, girls, come in.'

They'd tidy up, do our dishes, and service anyone in any way they required. But no one did anything that they didn't want to do. It was all consensual and good fun. The girls wanted to hang out with the band, and we loved having them around.

There were a few different groups of girls: the hardcore fans were the girls who would literally do anything for you. There was the sophisticated set, girls like Mary, who were friends of the band. And then there were the innocents, girls like Gabby. You knew where to go and where not to go; you didn't want any dramas.

Gab was just fourteen when I met her. I was nineteen. She was a beautiful, young, innocent girl, and I remember thinking, 'I'd hate to see her get into any trouble.' So, I kept an eye on her, to make sure she was okay, just like I did with the guys.

Of course, Gab and the other 'innocents' knew what was going on. Years later, she told me that she and Betty referred to the flat's front bedroom as 'The Bad Room'. They knew what was happening in that room, and it wasn't where they wanted to go.

Back then, groupies were unflatteringly called 'band molls'. Molly Meldrum asked Bon in *Go-Set*: 'Do you take advantage of band molls?'

'No, I don't,' Bon replied. 'But if I feel like it and there's something available, then why not?'

Why not, indeed?

The Valentines could be downright dirty, but because they played pop music, they didn't have a 'bad boy' image like The Masters Apprentices. The Masters were the antithesis of the 'Think Pink' Zoot. They caused a storm when singer Jim Keays talked about groupies in an interview with Lily Brett in *Go-Set* on 17 July 1968. The piece was headed: 'Sex Is Thrust On Us . . . We've Seen Too Many Bodies—Had Too Many Girls'.

'Three years in the pop business has taught me that many girls are potential band molls,' Jim said. 'About twenty girls a day come to our home. On Sunday, it averages fifty.

'I'll give you a typical example of what happens. Last week a girl walked in and said, "Right, who's going to make love to me first?" She used a rather more obscene expression than "make love".

'In Brisbane, a bird came into our hotel room. She took off all her clothes and said, "You can all have me, who wants to go first?"

'And only recently we were in a Victorian country town when five girls aged between fifteen and eighteen somehow got into our hotel room. They didn't say a word. They took their clothes off and said, "Will you judge and see which one of us has got the best breasts?" We couldn't very well take no notice of them, could we?'

Jim added: 'Back in the old days, we took advantage of the girls. We lashed out! Could you blame us? We came from a normal existence, where sex is reasonably hard to get, to suddenly having it thrust on us.'

Lily wrote: 'We at *Go-Set* deplore the facts of the story. We feel that there is little or no hope of eradicating the type of behaviour described, but we do hope that both pop stars and over-enthusiastic girl fans will think deeply about the facts of the matter.'

The story led to a backlash. Two months later, Jim hit back, telling *Go-Set*: 'All this publicity makes one feel like chucking the whole pop scene in at times. Lately, it's just been ridiculous. I've had threats on my life and we've been called sex maniacs and homosexuals. Boys want to beat me up at dances . . . If you're honest, it gets you nowhere. It seems that people don't want to read the truth.'

During the furore, someone wrote 'BAND MOLL'S PARADISE' in huge white letters outside Jim's flat in Carlisle Avenue, East St Kilda.

Jim later reflected, 'The more their parents hated us, the more the kids loved us.'

Jim could have been telling The Valentines' story. Sex was thrust on us . . . and we couldn't say no, could we?

Some girls didn't mind being in a room with everyone. I haven't been in an orgy since The Valentines days, but I had a few back then. Everyone and everything seemed free. It was no big deal. 'I'll just be having a root,' a band member would say. 'Cool, let me know when it's over, 'cause someone else might want one.'

And, of course, these were the pre-AIDS days. Sex couldn't kill you, though it could lead to some unpleasant trips to the VD clinic. In the late sixties, there was a group of girls who would go from The Valentines to the Zoot and The Masters Apprentices and even to the wrestlers at Festival Hall. Because of these girls, everyone caught the clap at the same time. It was nasty and inconvenient but just an occupational hazard. You'd head off to the VD clinic, get a jab in your bum and then return to your wicked ways.

Years later, Jim Keays from The Masters Apprentices told me that he would pretend to be a member of another band when he was at the VD clinic. The doctors knew he was in a band, but had no idea which one, so he'd tell them he was in The Valentines or Zoot, to avoid embarrassment. Only problem was the guys in The Valentines would tell the doctors they were in The Masters Apprentices!

Some girls were very good groupies. They would do crazy things. It was like they decided, 'If I'm going to be a groupie, I'm going to be the best.' You had to admire their commitment.

One of Australia's most infamous groupies was known as the Lithgow Leaper. Bon made a cryptic reference to her in a newspaper column during the AC/DC years. 'Can I send out a couple of cheerios?' he said. 'In Bathurst, a very rare animal—the Lithgow Leaper. Keep it up, mate.'

This 'very rare animal' was notorious for her phone-answering skills and what she could do with the receiver: 'You've called the Lithgow Leaper's answering cervix.'

Girls helped to make life on the road a lot of fun. When The Valentines toured Adelaide, the girls were waiting for us in the car park at the motel. Who told them we were coming? And how quickly could we run our bags upstairs and get down to business?

All the comforts of home.

You can understand why there was no way I was going to give up this lifestyle. But my time with The Valentines was nearly derailed when I was drafted to serve in Vietnam.

Darryl Sambell's political connections kept Johnny Farnham out of the draft. Ross Wilson was called up but got an exemption because he had a gammy leg, the result of being hit by a car when he was sixteen. Jim Keays pretended to be a bed-wetter to dodge the draft. But Normie Rowe wasn't so lucky. The King of Pop was called up in 1967. He served in Vietnam and never had another Top 40 hit.

There was no way I was going to go to Vietnam. This wasn't our war. My attitude was, 'If the Commies are coming here, we'll meet them here and fight them here.' Otherwise, it wasn't our fight. It was wrong to randomly pick guys to go to fight in a war at a crucial time in their lives.

I read an interview in *High Times* with American rocker Ted Nugent, who claimed that he dodged the draft by not washing for a month. He didn't change his clothes, shave or brush his teeth. And then a week before his medical, he stopped going to the toilet, preferring to piss and shit in his own pants. Desperate times call for desperate measures. The army sergeant called Ted a 'fucking swine'.

I didn't go quite as far as Ted, but I did everything I could to fail my medical. It started with the hearing test. You had to put your hand up when you heard the beeps. *Beep.* 'Yep.' *Beep.* 'Yep.' *Beep.* 'Yep.' *Beep, Beep, Beep.* 'Nah, I can't hear shit, mate. Nah, nothing.'

I also flunked my sight test. When they pointed at 'E', I said, 'Is it an F?'

Then I had to strip. I was naked with two guys in white coats poking and prodding me. I pretended to have no balance when they asked me to hop around. I told them I had asthma and bronchitis. 'And I think I've got syphilis.'

Soon after, we were doing a gig at Coburg Town Hall. My brother was waiting there for me, with a letter. *Shit,* I thought, *this will be my Vietnam letter. There's no way I'm going into the army. I'm going to have to do a runner.*

I nervously opened the envelope and saw the two most beautiful words in the English language: *Medically unfit.*

I could resume normal life.

At my sixtieth birthday, my good mate Mick Cox made a speech. I got to know Coxy during The Valentines days when he was Doug Parkinson's roadie.

'I first met Darcy when he was transporting seafood up and down the east coast,' Coxy said in his speech.

It was an in-joke and not many people got it. Coxy was referring to The Valentines tour that gave me a nasty dose of crabs. When we left Sydney, heading for Brisbane, someone mentioned that there was a bad case of crabs going around Sydney.

'What are crabs?' I asked, innocently.

By the time we arrived at the Indooroopilly Motel, I knew what crabs were. I had a shower and was then picking the crabs off my nuts with a pair of tweezers. The motel door flew open and in burst Coxy and Doug Parkinson. 'G'day, Darce, how ya going?'

It really was 'Make Love, Not War' back in those days. The sex, the drugs and the rock'n'roll were definitely full-on. But I must stress that no one was forced to do anything they didn't want to do. It was good, clean dirty fun.

COMMONWEALTH OF AUSTRALIA   NATIONAL SERVICE ACT 1951-1968

CERTIFICATE OF REGISTRATION

FULL NAME JOHN DENNIS   DARCY

1. You must immediately sign this Certificate in the place indicated and keep it as evidence of your registration. You may be required to produce it to persons authorized under the Act.
2. The Certificate must not be altered or defaced.
3. If the details shown on this Certificate are incorrect, or if your place of living changes from that shown in your registered address you must advise the Registrar below within 30 days and return this Certificate to him as indicated on the other side of this Certificate.
4. If you lose this Certificate, or if it is destroyed or defaced, you must report the fact forthwith to the Registrar below or to the District Officer at any District Office of the Commonwealth Employment Service.

Registered Address

MR J D DARCY
23 GALLIPOLI PDE
PASCOE VALE SOUTH VIC

USUAL SIGNATURE of Registered Person

Registration Number 21154896 Issued by Registrar at MELBOURNE Date 07/02/69

NS2(REV 12/67)

The unluckiest number—getting the call up for Vietnam.

The Valentines won Best Stage Act in Go-Set's *1969 Awards. Melbourne's leading DJ, Stan 'The Man' Rofe, wrote: 'Who are the two best young groups in this country? Silly question, easy answer. The Masters Apprentices and The Valentines. The Masters lead the field, The Valentines have yet to enter—a field of originality. It's a great pity The Valentines have taken so long to recognise their own song writing ability, which, if anything, is as good as the now defunct Easybeats. Don't wipe the Valis off despite their lack of records; 1970 could be their year.'*

It's a long way to the top

Darce

It was always a trip seeing Bon and the boys get ready for gigs or TV appearances. The flat would be packed with six guys all putting on their chiffon outfits. Hair permed, with sticky tape attached, trying to keep everything in place. It was a long way from the wild, uninhibited rock look that Bon would become known for.

Bon would also apply foundation to his arms, to hide his tattoos. It was a different scene back then—tattoos weren't a part of the pop world in the sixties. Only wharfies and bikies and criminals sported tattoos, and they didn't fit The Valentines' poppy image. I could sense Bon regretted getting his tattoos. He even told me he thought about getting them removed, which would have been a rather unpleasant process in 1969.

Bon's ink was still a bit of an issue during the AC/DC days. I remember Angus did an interview with Molly Meldrum on *Countdown* and Molly asked: 'There was this image when they talked about AC/DC of basically that tattoo of Bon, and you as a schoolboy; did that worry you?' Angus replied, 'As long as people were talking about us, great, even if it was bad.' But, of course, Bon's tattoos were much more suited to a rock band like AC/DC than a pop band like The Valentines.

That said, many of the gigs we did were at rough venues. Bon could certainly handle himself, but he wasn't a violent man and he never went looking for trouble. And part of my job was to be on the lookout for any potential trouble and make sure we avoided it. I didn't want my band getting into any fights.

One night we rocked up to a gig in Werribee, out in the south-western suburbs of Melbourne, where Zoot had been beaten up the week before. Bon was wearing a fur coat and red patent leather shoes. As I was unloading the guitars from the van, the band was walking into the venue and I could see the bouncers rubbing their hands together and then clenching their fists and nodding to each other.

'Hey,' I said, running up to the door, 'they're with me and I'm with them.'

'What are you doing with these poofters?'

'They ain't poofters, mate,' I replied, spelling out a fact. 'These guys will get more roots in a week than you'll get in your fucking life.'

'Can we get a job?' one of the bouncers smirked.

Fuck off!

We lived together, we toured together, we stuck up for each other. And, of course, we partied together. The parties at our Toorak Road flat were legendary. A few years ago, I caught up with Russell Morris on the Gold Coast. 'Mate,' he smiled, 'I'll never forget that night in Toorak Road!'

I used to be in charge of the light show at the parties. Someone had knocked off the projector from Bertie's, so we'd all get stoned and project tiny coloured balls onto the ceiling. Everyone would be lying on the floor as the colours filled the room. It was crazy hippie psychedelic shit.

Another night, when we were celebrating Ted's birthday, we all cracked up when a car crashed into a parked car out the front of our flat about 2.30 a.m. But our mate Harry stopped laughing when he realised it was his car. 'That's my fucking car,' Harry yelled, 'and I've got some shit in the glove box!' He had to run down and remove the gear before the cops arrived.

Life on the road was even more fun. We spent a lot of time in that little Ford Thames. We'd always do two gigs on a Thursday and a Friday, and then three or four on Saturdays, plus maybe a gig on Sunday afternoon and another one on Sunday night. We usually had Monday, Tuesday and Wednesday off, though we often did a lunchtime high school gig on Wednesdays.

For road trips, Bon would cook up a big batch of hash cookies, and Wyn would always carry the cookie jar. The cookies would give a nice little blast. On the road, we'd rip into the cookies and blow a few joints. The van would always be filled with smoke. Looking back, it wasn't the safest of working environments: six guys in a van, no seat belts, with amplifiers flying around. And often, I'd be running red lights to make sure we got to the next gig on time.

Nowadays, you'd call it an OH&S nightmare, but back then we didn't think like that. I did all the driving—I didn't trust anyone else. You could say I was stupid: I was out of control, but I was in control, if that makes sense. And by this stage, I'd decided to do the right thing and get my driver's licence!

After a couple of suburban gigs on a Saturday night, we'd always end up with a late show at a city club, like Bertie's, where the bouncer on the door had the most unbelievable hash. We'd have a 1 a.m. start in the basement and I'd have to make about twenty trips unloading the gear, going up and down the stairs. The bouncer had a falcon pipe filled with hash and he'd stick it in my mouth every time I walked past him, so I could have a little puff.

Sometimes I think the Bertie's crowd came to the gig just to see us set up. It must have been like a comedy routine because we were all so stoned. There was a little triangular stage, with a tiny band room at the back. Instead of the guys staying out the back, they'd be chatting to me and bumping into me on stage as I was trying to set up the gear. I'd be like, 'Get out the fucking back and wait till we're sorted!' Then the light in the back room would flick on and off, which was the venue's way of saying, 'Come on, it's time to start.'

I would often get a cheer when I was on stage setting up the band. The Valentines' young fans all got to know me. I remember Bill Joseph once said, 'We'll have to set up a fan club for Darcy.' Two young fans, Hilda and Mercy, actually gave me a pewter mug, which was inscribed: *Best Roadie Ever*. They were great girls. The joke was that you'd give it to Hilda and she would scream for Mercy.

They were fun, happy days, and Bon always loved doing gigs. No matter what state we were in, Bon would always manage to focus backstage. After a little bit of honey and some whisky, he was always ready to sing.

The cannabis scene in those days was a closed circuit—universities, music and theatre. We'd rock up to do a lunchtime show at a uni and be stopped by security at the gate. Then we'd go into the union building and it'd be filled with hippies smoking. We loved it.

Our longer road trips—usually between Melbourne and Sydney—were literally a trip, because we'd often drop acid. Some people would have one trip and go crazy; I had hundreds of trips and it never fazed me. That said, I did find myself in situations where I had to walk out of restaurants because the chicken was pulsating and the peas were rolling around.

If the band was smoking, I was smoking more than anyone. And if they were dropping trips, I was also doing it. But somehow, I learned to adapt and hold everything together. I had to get the band to the gigs, get them out safely and get them home. I think it helped that I didn't drink alcohol—I had abstained ever since I had suffered alcohol poisoning when I was fourteen.

When I hear AC/DC's early songs—tracks like 'The Jack', 'Show Business', 'Rock'n'roll Singer', 'Rocker', 'Ain't No Fun (Waiting Round To Be A Millionaire)' and especially 'It's A Long Way To The Top'—I know that I lived those songs with Bon.

We were ripped off. We got stoned. We were underpaid. And, yes, it's harder than it looks. But that's show business, know what I mean? And we also had the time of our lives.

We'd be gigging in another city away from home and when the promoter was due to pay us, he would have disappeared. So, I'd have to call our manager and say, 'Bill, can you send up some money? We need to get home.' Once, we were stranded in Brisbane when our van blew up. My mate Scrooge—who went on to become the roadie for Daddy Cool and Little River

Band—organised for our equipment to be sent home on a bus. Bon, Paddy and I also got on the bus, while the rest of the band flew home.

At every roadhouse stop, we'd jump off, whip around the side and get a smoke on. The hooch helped us deal with a shitty trip.

On another interstate trip, we ran out of petrol on the highway just as dawn was breaking. We all fell out of the van; I was so out of it, I struggled to pour the petrol from the jerry can into the tank. Then as we got back into the van, I realised one band member was missing. 'Where the fuck is Bon?' I looked across the highway to see him rolling in a field of grass, dressed in a long coat that was like a pleated bedspread with a hood. The truckies were tooting their horns—they thought he was a chick, this strange vision in their rear view mirror.

That remains my favourite image of Bon.

Bon always carried a little pocket-sized Spirax notebook, and in it he jotted down song ideas and potential titles. He started writing towards the end of The Valentines, including the band's final single, a ballad called 'Juliette'. I didn't really dig the song, but every writer has to start somewhere.

When The Valentines performed 'Juliette' live, it used to piss Bon off when Vince would do a harmony on the 'Juliette' line. Bon would be so immersed in the song and then Vince's voice would ruin it for him.

Our life on the road gave Bon plenty of material to work with. When you're in an unfriendly country town, it's a case of, 'Mate, we're the only fuckers in this town who know each other, we have to stick together.' After a gig in Shepparton, in country Victoria, we were literally run out of town. The gig, at the Civic Centre, actually went pretty well—the joint was rocking—but for some reason, half-a-dozen locals wanted to fight us after the show.

The local copper pointed to the road and said simply: 'Melbourne's that way, fellas.' We got the hint, and I drove out of there as fast as I could, with the locals pounding on the van.

We never knew what awaited us on the road. One young lady, a regular at the Toorak Road flat, turned up to one of our Sydney gigs, having driven from Melbourne with her mother. During the show, I was standing at the mixing desk when the woman came up to me. 'My mother wants to see you,' she said.

'Hang on,' I replied, 'we're in the middle of a gig.'

After the show, while I was loading the amps into the van as we prepared to race to another show, the girl confronted me again. She was pregnant and trying to tell me that the kid was mine. The mother was talking to Vince; she had the hots for Vince and he seemed keen. He was always up for the challenge: *I've had the daughter, I'll get the mother . . .*

Me? I just wanted to get out of there. 'Listen,' I said, 'why are you saying it's mine? You've been with all the others!' I loaded up the van and drove off.

You had to laugh.

On another occasion, a girl and her sister turned up to our house, pushing a baby in a pram. I was sitting in the lounge room with a couple of mates when Gab appeared. She didn't look happy. She elbowed me and said, 'There's someone at the door who wants to see you.'

The girl was claiming that the kid was mine. But it wasn't. Fortunately, Gab has always been my number one supporter.

'It's not his,' Gab told the girl. 'And if you don't fuck off, I'll push you off this verandah.'

Thanks, Gab!

Our kids, Bec and Matt, have always thought that a half-brother or sister might one day turn up on our doorstep. Who knows if Bon has any kids out there? According to Michael Browning, Bon boasted that he once visited two women in the same maternity ward, after both had given birth to his kids—unbeknown to each other. Sounds like a tall story to me, but anything is possible. I never thought Vince was overly handsome, but he managed to have five children to five different women.

During The Valentines days, we got to know a young guy named Michael Gudinski. He'd been running some dances at Caulfield Town Hall while he was still at school. Then he started working with our manager, Bill Joseph. Michael used to come around to our flat to discuss band business. He would always stand back when we were smoking. You could tell that he thought we were wild boys.

We liked Michael straightaway. He was obviously a smart kid and he was eager to learn. To further his education, he decided to accompany The Valentines on a trip to Adelaide. He wanted to see how a band functioned on the road. It was Michael Gudinski's first tour.

In Adelaide, we did a store promotion at Myer, which was a great way to meet the local young ladies. We took them all back to our motel. I still remember the look of shock on Michael's face when our motel room soon resembled a Roman orgy.

'So, this is how it goes on the road?' he inquired.

'Well, Michael, it's the old saying,' I said with a wink, *'What goes on the road, stays on the road.'*

In August 1969, The Valentines were part of 'Operation Starlift', a massive Australian tour that also involved The Masters Apprentices, Johnny Farnham, Zoot, Johnny Young and Ronnie Burns. Unfortunately, the promoter, Ron Blackmore, told me that my services were not required—the tour already had enough roadies. So, I stayed home and partied with Bon's brother, Graeme, at the Toorak Road flat. We had a lot of fun, but I also missed a crazy tour.

At the beginning of the tour, The Masters' guitarist, Doug Ford, announced the Operation Starlift competition: to see who could score the most points 'for despicable and dirty deeds'.

'But I must warn you that if I hear good things about anybody,' Doug said, 'they automatically lose points. For example, if I hear a girl say, "Gee, Ronnie Burns is a nice guy", Ron will lose five points. On the other hand, if I hear a girl say that Vince Lovegrove was nothing but a pig, Vince will earn five points . . . six if she was crying. Remember, originality is the key note. I'll want to hear of everyone's exploits. May the best man win.'

Such is life on the road when you put a bunch of boys together.

Glenn Wheatley recounted some of the gory details in his book *Paper Paradise*. After day one, Bon was on top with thirty-two points. And he didn't relinquish his lead. Announcing the winner at the end of the tour, Jim Keays said, 'I'm afraid after that first night in Hobart, it was just Bon all the way.' When Bon got up to accept his award, he thanked what was in his hands—a large vibrator, 'without which I would not be here receiving this award tonight'.

'Operation Starlift' was an important tour in Australian rock history. It was also a turning point in Glenn Wheatley's life, convincing him that he was better off behind the scenes. Glenn, who was the bass player in The Masters Apprentices at the time, discovered that the rock stars might have had the most fun, but managers and promoters made the most money.

At Brisbane's Festival Hall, Ron Blackmore came running backstage to inform The Masters that they'd set a new record.

'It's a bigger crowd than The Beatles!' he exclaimed.

More than 7000 screaming kids were at the show. A decade later, Jim Keays was watching Saturday morning pop show *Sounds*, with host Donnie Sutherland interviewing Doc Neeson, who revealed: 'We've just been up in Brisbane, where we played Festival Hall and broke The Masters Apprentices' record.'

Jim's ears pricked up. He rang The Angels' manager, John Woodruff. 'John, I don't want to know your business,' he said, 'but I was just interested—what was your deal for the Festival Hall show?'

'Well,' said John, doing the sums in his head, 'it was ten bucks to get in, and we got seven of every ten. So, all up, it was about fifty grand.'

'Do you wanna know what we got when we set the record?' Jim asked John.

'Well,' John pondered, 'things were a little different in those days, so you probably only got about five grand.'

'No,' Jim said, 'we got fifty bucks.'

Bands in the sixties were definitely doing it for the girls and good times—there certainly wasn't a lot of cash floating around. Fortunately, musicians like Glenn Wheatley learned all the lessons and helped artists get a bigger slice of the pie in the seventies and eighties.

After another Valentines tour to Adelaide, the band flew to Sydney while I drove the van back to Melbourne to get the amplifiers fixed. Then I had to load up the van again and head to Sydney, where I was to meet Bon and Paddy at a house in Paddington.

I was smoking and sniffing speed along the way, and as I crossed the NSW border I started to hallucinate. I can remember it clearly, thought I was losing my mind. I was seeing misty faces in the trees overhanging the road. I was starting to freak out, and I was talking to myself: 'Get it together!'

I ended up pulling over in a rest spot. In the Ford Thames, the motor is tucked in beside you, so I put my head down on the engine cover for a little break. I'm not sure how long I dozed off—maybe ten minutes or half an hour, I'm not sure—but I shot up all of a sudden to be greeted by a misty figure. It was Paddy. 'Where's Bon?' I said. 'We gotta go!'

I looked outside and saw a misty figure of Bon, jumping around and laughing. 'Stop fucking around and get in the van!' I ordered. I turned on the ignition and got back on the Hume Highway, hugging the steering wheel all the way to Sydney. When I finally arrived at the big bluestone house belonging to a couple of girls who were putting us up, I walked down the hallway and found Bon in the kitchen, making a bong out of a milk bottle.

'Mate, we've been waiting for you,' he said. 'Where have you been?'

'You won't believe what I've gone through.'

I'd been awake for days.

Our plan was to head straight to Brisbane, but Bon had the hots for Carol, who worked at one of the Sydney clubs, Caesars, and he gave me a wink and said, 'Can we stick around till lunchtime?'

I then discovered that the van had a flat tyre, and we didn't have a jack. And, of course, the spare tyre was also flat.

'Let's leave after tea,' Bon suggested.

'After tea' became 10 p.m., then 11.30. Then Bon wanted to see Carol before we left. It was about 1 a.m. before we hit the road. I was wired.

Bon and Paddy were asleep on the speaker boxes in the back of the van. I was also starting to nod off, and suddenly I ran off the road and hit the gravel. Bon and Paddy shot up like a couple of meerkats.

'What was that?'

'Nothing,' I said. 'Go back to sleep.'

When the sun came up, I pulled into a service station at Warwick, south of Brisbane. I opened the door and just fell onto the driveway, with my arms and legs in the air.

'I'm fucked, mate,' I said, as Bon got out of the van. 'I can't go any further. I took out a post back there.'

So, Bon drove us into Brisbane.

Later that afternoon, I unpacked the boxes and found that the post I'd hit had come through underneath the van, jammed into the diff and punched a hole in the floor. If it had come through the speaker boxes that Bon and Paddy were lying on, it would have killed both of them.

That was my worst trip. But it was all part of rock'n'roll.

Packing up after a gig at Lucifer's in Melbourne's CBD.
A couple of fans checking out Darce's style.

Touring with The Flying Circus and Johnny Farnham. Bon and Darce backstage
at Casino in NSW in 1969, hanging out with Jim Wynne, lead singer of The
Flying Circus. The promoter and his wife were filming and turned a spotlight
on us—which we didn't handle too well as we were pretty stoned. Jim turned
out to be an amazing artist and his work was hung in the National Gallery.

In an interview with the American edition of Rolling Stone *magazine in 1978, to promote the US release of AC/DC's album* Powerage, *Bon mentioned that he was impressed by how Frank Zappa had been able to manipulate his image over the years, citing the PHI ZAPPA KRAPPA poster of Frank sitting on the toilet. Bon suggested his own version: 'Bon Scott pulling himself.'*

Busted!

Darce

In September 1969, things were changing in The Valentines. The bass player, John Cooksey, was leaving, and the band decided to downsize, with Ted, the rhythm guitarist, switching to bass. To rehearse the new line-up, the guys booked the surf lifesaving club at Jan Juc, 100 kilometres out of Melbourne.

I packed all the gear and loaded everyone into the van, each with our own bag of smoke. When we arrived at the club I couldn't believe how barren the area was: there were no shops; in fact, you couldn't see a house for miles.

'Fucked if I'm staying here for a week,' I declared. 'I'm going to drive back to Melbourne and I'll come back next Saturday and pick you up.'

I returned to the Toorak Road flat and hung out with Cooksey. He and I had the smoke—and the band's chicks—to ourselves for the week. Cooksey loved the ladies, probably a little too much. I liked Cooksey, but he wasn't always the best person to smoke with. He looked like an old man with long hair, and he also had long fingernails. When we got stoned, he looked like a witch, which always freaked me out a little.

While we were hanging out, something strange happened. As I was blowing a big, fat joint, I looked out the window and spotted an unmarked police car. I'd had some dealings with the cops during my younger years, and they stood out like dog's balls. They were watching our flat.

'Fuck, what's going on here?'

Later on, it was a different car. Again I stood at the window, blowing my joint, watching the cops.

Come Saturday, I jumped in the van and headed to Jan Juc, to pick up the boys. When I arrived, they were running around like headless chooks. Vince was panicking. 'You haven't got any shit on you, have you? Get rid of the shit—we've been busted!'

'I'm not getting rid of it,' I replied. 'It's good buds, mate!'

'Let's get back to Melbourne—we've got to get a lawyer.'

The guys were freaking out. They had no idea what was going to happen. They were worried what our manager, Bill Joseph, would say. It might be the end of the band. This was heavy!

Bon filled me in on what had happened. After a long day rehearsing, the guys put down their instruments about 10 p.m., lit up a smoke and put on some records. About half an hour later, there was a knock on the door—it was the CIB and they had a search warrant. They found a pipe and an envelope containing a small quantity of marijuana.

The Valentines were the first Australian band to be busted for drugs. They were fingerprinted at the Russell Street police headquarters. It was big news in 1969. Back then, the cops were clueless when it came to dope. And most people thought marijuana was something you injected.

A public notice was run in the pop press, featuring a picture of a cigarette and a teapot. 'Beware!' it screamed. 'This may be handed to you by a friendly stranger. It contains the killer drug Marihuana—a powerful narcotic in which lurks Murder! Insanity! Death!

'Warning! Drug peddlers are shrewd. They put some of this drug in the [tea pot] or in the tobacco cigarette.'

Crazy days.

The Valentines had already had a few minor issues with the law. A week before news of the bust broke, *Go-Set* ran a piece headed 'Valentines Versus The Cops'. By the end of the sixties, anyone with long hair was a target for the police. 'What about the time I was taken in for swearing in the street, or something equally stupid,' Bon said. 'And the first thing they [the police] wanted to do was to cut my hair! They just can't stand to see anyone look different from what they think is right.

'They should realise that what we do is right for us . . . We respect a lot of things about their job, but they shouldn't persecute whole groups of people just for being different.'

Vince also had some advice for the boys in blue: 'They should concentrate a bit on catching real criminals, not just kids they suspect of breaking the law. And it seems all you have to do to be a suspect is to have long hair and wear gear clothes.'

The bust gave The Valentines a bad-boy image, but it also cost us a lot of bookings. Teachers and parents no longer wanted us to play at schools, the ABC was reluctant to book us on the telly, and the Immigration Department even threatened to send Paddy back to New Zealand.

Before he heard that we'd been busted, Molly filed his column for that week's edition of *Go-Set*. He wrote about 'the happy Valentines', stating: 'This group has proved us all wrong—me in particular. In the last six months they have managed to put life back into the charts . . . there is no stopping The Valentines now.'

The night before news of the bust broke, Vince called Mitch at *Go-Set* in what would now be called damage control. She reported that he was 'highly distraught', and when asked if the Valentines smoked dope, Vince admitted, 'Over the past two or three months, we have had the occasional smoke . . . I guess it started when we read that groups such as The Beatles and the Stones "smoked".'

And Vince had a message for the paper's young readers. 'Let what has happened to us be a warning to others. Smoking is just not worth the risk of wrecking your career.

'We have a lot of faith in our fans . . . all we can do is hope this won't turn them against us. We all make mistakes at some time in our life and what really matters is that we learn from our experience.'

Vince was particularly concerned about the drug charges because he was already on a good-behaviour bond after a little drama during The Valentines' Moomba concert in 1969. During the show the cops had thrown a girl off the stage, and Vince had got into a scuffle with them, ending with him being charged with assaulting police and using indecent language.

This was serious stuff, so the band made a pact: no more smoking. Bon gave up for a day; I was never going to stop. But Ted and Wyn quit for three months—until they caught Bon, Paddy and me having a secret puff. 'You arseholes!' they bellowed. We used to call Wyn and Ted 'Grandma and Grandpa' because they were the voice of reason in the band—not that we ever listened.

After the band's court appearance, Vince called for a law change. 'Something could be done to partly legalise smoking marijuana in supervised centres, like hotels,' he suggested. 'People with a licence could smoke. And it could be legalised for adults in their own homes.'

The Valentines appeared in Geelong Court in February 1970. The guys pleaded guilty and were represented by Mr William Lennon, who told the court that it was a conspiracy—one of our rivals in the pop world had tipped off the drug squad. 'Somebody in the entertainment world was ill-disposed to them,' he said.

But this is how it actually happened . . .

A few weeks before the bust, a young girl knocked on the door of our flat. She was an art student selling paintings. Now, we weren't necessarily art connoisseurs, but we invited her in. After a few minutes, Bon appeared, wearing just his red jocks and carrying a tray of cookies. Bon had been cooking in the kitchen, but this wasn't his best batch—the cookies had all fused together and were a strange yellowy-green colour. But the girl was keen to try one, and we also made her a cup of tea.

About ten minutes later, she asked, 'What have you guys done to me?' She realised that the cookies weren't of the choc-chip variety. She laughed and then enjoyed a joint with us, before departing.

We didn't buy any of her paintings.

Soon after, the girl wrote a letter to her sister in Adelaide, revealing how she'd smoked a joint with The Valentines.

Unfortunately, the girl's sister and her housemates were raided by the South Australian cops, who found the letter. They tipped off their Victorian counterparts . . . and that's how The Valentines were busted in Jan Juc.

Mr Lennon tried to justify our smoking to the court. 'The group have told me that under the influence of marijuana they became more perceptive to musical sounds.' He also said we'd been influenced by the drug use of The Beatles and The Rolling Stones. 'Youthful curiosity and the life in the world of discotheques and drug taking were the reasons for it.'

The Valentines rocked up to court in long frock coats and bell-bottomed trousers, with long pointed shirt collars, wide ties and long hair. 'They appear before you in far-out costumes and long hair,' our lawyer told the magistrate, 'but it is part of the mystique of their business. Underneath it, they are responsible and decent young people.'

The magistrate bought it, and fined the guys just $150 each and put them all on good-behaviour bonds, with Vince's good-behaviour bond extended for another twelve months.

It was a good result and we had a smoke to celebrate.

While The Valentines were off in Jan Juc near Torquay getting busted for drugs, the party continued back at Toorak Road. The police spent a lot of time watching from the street. Left to right: Gab, Graeme Scott, Sue and Tess (who came over from Perth to visit the boys), Darce and Betty King.

The end of the beginning

Darce

The Valentines weren't going to last forever. We were having fun, but you could tell that musically, the band wasn't where Bon wanted to be.

I'd like to think that Paddy and I helped to influence Bon's music tastes. When we arrived, The Valentines were still like an Aussie version of The Monkees—it was a teenybopper trip. But Paddy and I introduced them to Hendrix, Zeppelin and Traffic.

In 1969, we toured Perth. It was the first time the band had been home in a couple of years. They'd had some national exposure, so they were homecoming heroes. It was a big deal, and it seemed like the whole town came out to greet them. It was like we were The Beatles at the airport, with hundreds of kids chasing us. As I started running, Wyn yelled, 'What about the bags?'

'Fuck the bags,' I replied. 'Let's get outta here!'

The boys lapped up the attention, from the media and the fans, and Bon managed to combine the two when we did a live-to-air interview at a local radio station. As the guys answered the probing questions, Bon was probing a young lady on the floor.

Just before we left Melbourne, I'd bought Led Zeppelin's debut album, which I'd imported through a little shop in South Yarra. I didn't even have a chance to play the record before we headed for the airport. In Perth, Vince's folks gave him one of the early model cassette players, so he recorded the Zeppelin vinyl on to tape.

When we flew back to Melbourne, there was some mix-up with the tickets and I ended up in first class, while the band was in economy. 'See ya, boys!' I said as I headed for the front of the plane, in my ripped T-shirt, jeans and moccasins. All I could hear from my first-class seat was the Led Zeppelin album blaring from Vince's tape player in economy.

The Perth trip was also the first time I heard Santana's debut album—it was at one of the radio stations when we did an interview. Bon loved those Zeppelin and Santana albums, particularly the groove of Santana. It was the first time we'd heard a band sound really free. They would break out of the constraints of a three-minute song and improvise and jam in the middle. Bon loved it so much he bought a set of timbales.

Though Bon's music tastes might have been expanding, his fashion sense stayed the same. The Valentines' flash stage outfits were never Bon's style. If he could, he would have lived his entire life in just a pair of shorts, a singlet and bare feet. Of course, many venues would not allow a barefoot Bon inside, so we were forever shopping for thongs. I remember one trip to Sydney in 1969. As always, Bon needed some thongs, so we ended up at Coles in the city. We noticed some Skippy the Bush Kangaroo T-shirts, and Bon bought me one. I still have it.

Towards the end of 1969, The Valentines really started to mix things up. The band would dress up and do their 'teenybopper' show at suburban gigs, before ditching their flashy gear and putting on jeans and T-shirts for a late-night city gig. And they started to insert some cool covers into the set, including a version of Zeppelin's 'Communication Breakdown', as well as songs by Chicago and Blood, Sweat & Tears.

Go-Set's issue of 20 December 1969 featured an article by Jean Gollan, headed 'The New Look Valentines . . . Caught In The Act At Bertie's'. Jean wrote that the band had realised that trends were changing and they needed to cater for a 'more adult' audience. 'The Valentines are leading the way with their type of pop music,' she concluded, 'and they deserve to be the top pop group of 1970.'

We could do a teenybopper show in the afternoon with Zoot or The Masters, and then do a club gig that night, supporting Doug Parkinson or Thorpie. We had both scenes covered, and no one else could match us. The guys no longer wanted to be seen as a 'bubblegum' band. But as any artist will tell you, it's not easy to reinvent yourself. Just as Zoot struggled to shake their 'Think Pink—Think Zoot' image, The Valentines couldn't really break free from the bubblegum tag.

'We're still very image-conscious,' Vince told *Go-Set* in May 1970. 'But it's no longer a fabricated one. Now we just want to be ourselves.'

Bon, however, conceded that an image switch wasn't easy. 'The hardest thing for us is to live bubblegum down.'

Whenever we were on the road in Sydney, Adelaide or Brisbane, we'd go to the clubs to see Thorpie or Lobby Loyde or Doug Parkinson or Python Lee Jackson, and Bon would always get up and jam with them. He was forever up for shaking a tambourine, banging on the bongos or having a sing.

We loved Sydney because we started to pull a more mature crowd, including some older chicks. I remember one took me to Bondi Beach and rubbed me with coconut oil. It was pleasurable until about twenty minutes later when I resembled a lobster. And that night's gig was a nightmare—carrying the amps on my shoulder tore my red, raw skin to shreds.

I also celebrated my twenty-first birthday in Sydney with The Valentines. Bon signed my card: 'May you allways [sic] have: Peace, Happiness, Love & Rat Shit—Bon'.

Wyn added: 'May the god of love drop shit all over you, and forever live in eternal rat-shit.'

It sounds rude, but the messages were an in-joke. 'Rat-shit' was one of our favourite words at the time. Whenever we were stoned—which was rather often—we'd ask each other, 'How ya going?'

And the response would invariably be, 'I'm rat-shit, man.'

We were still having lots of fun, but it was obvious that The Valentines could no longer musically satisfy Bon, and the guys were drifting apart. Bon was sick of sharing a stage with Vince, knowing that Vince really couldn't cut it as a lead singer. Vince was more of a promoter and manager than an entertainer, whereas Bon was emerging as a songwriter and a great singer and entertainer.

The Valentines' final single was Bon's 'Juliette', released in February 1970. This was probably the band's finest musical moment. 'Valentines deserve a hit,' Ed Nimmervoll declared in *Go-Set*. 'The simplicity of "Nick Nack Paddy Wack" gives way to a more complex and far more ambitious project.'

Unfortunately, radio was reluctant to play 'Juliette', saying that the song was 'too slow'. 'It's not up to us to make hit records,' a 3UZ DJ told *Go-Set*. 'Our job is to play them once they are hits.' 'Juliette' sold well, but 3UZ and 3XY still wouldn't play it.

The band had gone as far as it could.

'Juliette' ended up reaching number twenty-eight on *Go-Set*'s national chart; it was the band's second-biggest hit.

In March 1970, just weeks before the end of The Beatles, The Valentines were forced to deny they were breaking up. The rumours started flying when people noticed a tiny classified ad in *Go-Set*: 'Valentines' equipment for sale', including speakers, amps, a Gibson guitar and a Fender bass. Stories started circulating that we were going overseas, or that Bon and Wyn were leaving to start a new band. Vince was forced to explain that we'd simply received some new gear as part of a sponsorship deal with Strauss. 'If the group was going to break up, *Go-Set* readers would be the first to know,' he said.

At the end of 1969, Vince and Bon did an interview with *The Herald*'s Tony Johnston. TJ talked about a planned LP and a trip to America, stating: 'Bon believes they could succeed there with a good record in their pack and plenty of good luck.' But the album and US tour never happened. That dream would have to wait for another band.

The Valentines never got to release an album; just seven singles. When it ended, it just ended. There was no big announcement or farewell tour. It wasn't like, 'Oh, we'll play in Melbourne, then Adelaide and then Perth.' It was just, 'This Sunday's the last one.'

'Their passing will leave a gap in the Australian pop scene which will be hard to fill,' *Go-Set* stated in a piece headed 'Last of the Teeny Groups?'.

'We've done as much as we can as The Valentines,' Vince explained. 'We've come to an age where we all have different ambitions. If we were to change the image of The Valentines to suit ourselves now, we'd need five different images.'

Stan Rofe was disappointed by the news. 'Are my ears on straight? Dear stupid Valentines, why the split? Surely you know you had a second to none chance of winning this year's national Battle of the Sounds?' Just after The Valentines split, The Flying Circus, representing New South Wales, won the Hoadley's title. Molly Meldrum called it 'an unpopular decision'. Zoot came second.

In *Go-Set's* 1970 Pop Poll, The Valentines came in at number six in the Best Australian Group section, just behind Zoot at number five. The Masters Apprentices took the title, ahead of Axiom, the band featuring former Valentines drummer Doug Lavery.

The final Valentines gig was in Werribee, on 2 August 1970. The place was packed and it was a great gig, but we had mixed emotions. We hadn't really come to terms with it at the time, but we knew that a great period in our lives was coming to an end.

Afterwards, we came back into town to Bill Joseph's office, which was in Russell Street, opposite the police station. Around 2 a.m., we had some smokes and a few drinks and started telling Bill about some of the things we'd done during our time together—which freaked him out because he hadn't realised he'd been managing a bunch of fucking yahoos. One of our vans had blown up in Brisbane, and we'd just left it at the motel; over time Bill had repeatedly asked Vince if he'd sorted it out, to which Vince had always replied, 'Yeah, yeah, we got rid of it.'

Bill ended up stuck with eighteen months' worth of parking fines because of that van. When The Valentines finished, every band member owed Bill money. Nearly four decades later, I bumped into Bill at a gig in Frankston and he told me that Bon was the only person to pay him back. Bill was a fantastic manager. No matter what happened to us, he always took care of us. A lot of other managers would just vanish when their clients needed help, and the cheque would always bounce, but never Bill.

To say thank you, on the night The Valentines played their final gig, we left Bill in his office with a couple of naked chicks—we'd thrown their clothes out the window, into the car park below.

Bon didn't seem distraught when The Valentines finished. He didn't have another band to go to, but he knew that rock'n'roll was his life and good things would happen.

As Vince would later reflect, 'The Valentines were never a great band . . . the emphasis was on entertainment.' But they were a good band, and it was like an apprenticeship for Bon.

Bon during The Valentines' last ever gig in Werribee. It was only decided a couple of days before that this would actually be the last gig, so there was no fanfare. Even Bill Joseph was taken by surprise.

Bon's voice inspired rock stars young and old. Smashing Pumpkins singer Billy Corgan said, 'Bon Scott sang every line like it was his last.' Lemmy from Motorhead was another fan. 'He was great, Bon. He had that voice . . . it sounded like he was fucking somebody while he was singing.'

Road-test Ronnie

Darce

During The Valentines, Bon loved catching up with other bands. He was always up for a jam or to just hang out. One of the bands he became friendly with was called Levi Smith's Clefs. Four members of that band ended up forming a new band called Fraternity in 1970, and bass player Bruce Howe asked Bon if he'd like to be their lead singer.

Go-Set summed up the mood when the band was starting at the end of 1970. 'It's a change in the air, the feeling that something is going to happen. If you're an optimist, it could even be that Australia is finally going onto the music map. If it is that, then a lot of credit will be due to Fraternity.'

Bon was positive, as always, but I could tell that he'd been scarred somewhat by the commercial frustrations of The Valentines years. 'Things seem to be looking good,' Bon said in November 1970, as Fraternity embarked on recording their debut album. 'But we won't be happy until we see the album moving in the States. There's so much garbage spouted about what people are going to do for you—and often it doesn't come off. We're waiting until the American people give their verdict before we start shouting really loudly.'

After The Valentines' failure to make it overseas, Bon was desperate to take his music to the US.

Fraternity started in Sydney, but soon based themselves in Adelaide. Vince Lovegrove—who became Adelaide's *Go-Set* correspondent when The Valentines finished—broke the news of the move at the end of December. 'Top Sydney group Fraternity announced this week that they will be making their base in Adelaide as from January 4, 1971.' Vince reported that the band didn't like the 'pace' of Sydney and they thought that Adelaide 'had all the possibilities of being Australia's Nashville'.

There was actually more to the move than the band let on. Their manager—a young Adelaide car dealer and entrepreneur named Hamish Henry—was funding the move to Adelaide and planning to pay the band a weekly wage for three years until they conquered the world.

'Our backers have asked to keep their names out of it,' Bon told *Go-Set*'s Greg Quill in an article headed 'A Farm, An Album, An American Tour—Will The Experiment Work?'.

Drummer John Freeman explained that Hamish's company viewed Fraternity as 'an economic investment'.

'If their investment doesn't pay off by then [three years], the party's over.'

Fraternity planned to tour the US by March 1971, where they had signed a deal with MCA. The band claimed to have received a telegram from MCA vice-president Dick Broderick in which he said he was 'absolutely knocked out by your talent'.

Bruce Howe was a little sceptical, saying in *Go-Set*, 'It's all just too good to believe.'

But Bon told him to 'quit worrying . . . there's no way in the world it can't work'.

With Bon based in Adelaide and fully focused on Fraternity, aside from letters and the occasional visit, we relied on *Go-Set* to keep in touch with what he was up to.

It was certainly a big change in Bon's life, going from living in a flat in Melbourne to a farm outside Adelaide, and switching from The Valentines' bubblegum pop to Fraternity's progressive rock.

Vince Lovegrove became Fraternity's number one supporter, regularly writing about the band in *Go-Set*. 'Fraternity live like no other band in Australia, in a house in the hills 17 miles from Adelaide. Surrounded by seven acres of bushland, they're secluded from everything but nature. What a buzz!'

Vince said the band 'only leave their pad to play gigs'.

The guys in Fraternity called Bon 'Road-test Ronnie'. 'If anyone came around with dubious substances, we'd give them to Bon,' John Freeman explained. 'If he was all right in a couple of hours, we'd all get into it. Bon would take anything.'

In June 1971, Vince tipped big things for Fraternity: 'In 15 months they will be one of the ten best bands in the world.'

Hamish Henry—who had a company called Music Power—was also behind the Myponga Festival. Sunbury is viewed as Australia's version of Woodstock, but Myponga happened a full year before the Victorian event. Held over three days in 1971—30 and 31 January and 1 February—on a farm 35 miles out of Adelaide, it was billed as the 'First Australian Festival of Progressive Music'. A three-day ticket cost $6. This was a hefty price for punters in 1971—Pink Floyd also toured Australia that year, and tickets cost $4—but it was worth every cent.

The festival's first announcement about the line-up included Cat Stevens, Daddy Cool, Sons of the Vegetal Mother, Company Caine, Healing Force, Spectrum, Chain, Billy Thorpe, Wendy Saddington and Fraternity. And Black Sabbath, featuring Ozzy Osbourne, were later added to the bill. 'Thirty hours on a plane sounded freaky, so we came,' said the singer, whom the Australian music press referred to by his real name: John Osbourne. Cat Stevens never actually made it to Myponga—he missed his plane in London—but the punters didn't seem to mind.

The festival's promotional flyer summed up the times: 'The promoters believe that in keeping with world trends of freedom of expression and thought in all fields of art, literature and music, Myponga 71 will be an exciting, aesthetic and elevating experience through progressive music.'

Fraternity played just before Black Sabbath on the Sunday night, but Ozzy had no idea he had shared a stage with Bon Scott until he was alerted to the fact a few decades later.

Gab and I went to Myponga with our roadie mate Scrooge, who was working with Daddy Cool. It was great to catch up with Bon, who rode his motorbike to the show. No one would get on the bike with Bon, apart from Gab—she had no fear!

Myponga was a lot of fun, summed up by one Adelaide paper in a report headed 'Bye Bye Bra', which stated that the festival had 'turned into the biggest exposé of the "no bra" look yet seen in South Australia'.

'There are about 2500 girls at the festival and there does not seem to be a bra between them,' the reporter wrote. 'The male pop lovers are dividing their time between the big sound on stage and the females.'

Bon, of course, had a great time.

(If you want to catch a glimpse of Myponga, check out Daddy Cool's classic clip for 'Eagle Rock'—the live footage was shot at Myponga, not Sunbury as most people assumed.)

Not long after Myponga, Fraternity released a new single, their cover of Blackfeather's 'Seasons of Change'. The members of the two bands had become friends in Sydney, and Bon had actually played the recorder on the Blackfeather version, which was on their debut album, *At The Mountains of Madness*. Bruce Howe asked Blackfeather's John Robinson if Fraternity could also record the song and he told them to go for it because Blackfeather didn't plan to release the song as a single.

'Seasons of Change' hit number one on the Adelaide charts and it was a highlight of Fraternity's set when they toured Melbourne in June 1971, playing at Bertie's, the Q Club and Opus.

With the Fraternity version taking off, Blackfeather's record company, Festival, changed their mind and decided to release the original version as a single. *Go-Set*'s Ed Nimmervoll called the move 'really silly'—he knew that only one version of the song would be a national hit. Unfortunately for Fraternity, Blackfeather were the winners, with their version of 'Seasons of Change' reaching number fifteen on *Go-Set*'s national chart. Fraternity's cover peaked at fifty-one. 'It was stupid,' Bruce Howe reflected. 'We're only cutting each other's throats.'

Bon embraced life on the farm. He was used to communal living, having lived with six other blokes in our flat during The Valentines days, though it was strange seeing him with a beard. 'We are satisfying ourselves and others by creating an environment,' Bon told *Go-Set* in 1971. There's no doubt that

Australia was a few years behind the rest of the world. The Swinging Sixties didn't really hit Australia until the seventies, around the same time the hippie movement kicked in. 'The point is the dollar sign is not the ultimate,' Bon claimed. 'We want to try to help each other develop and live.'

I was a little surprised when I read these comments, because Bon had never really been a hippie during his time with The Valentines. But, on the other hand, for Bon it was always about the music and the good times; the experience was much more important to him than money.

Fraternity were like an Australian version of The Band. They lived together and they toured together, occasionally taking their pet rabbit, Mervyn, along for the ride.

John Freeman added to Fraternity's hippie vibe, saying: 'We believe in our music, sure. But, more important, we believe in the people around us. We believe in that more than the almighty dollar. We're trying to get an environment happening and that's something that has never existed in Australian rock.'

Vince even got caught up in the Fraternity vibe, concluding his article: 'They are living as *human beings* and that's something we all need lessons in.'

Daddy Cool were the new kings of the Australian rock scene in 1971. They came in at number one in *Go-Set*'s prestigious Pop Poll. Blackfeather were at number ten. Fraternity didn't make the Top 10.

After their Melbourne shows in mid-1971, Fraternity headed to Queensland, where Bon had another run-in with the law. While on stage at a Surfers Paradise hotel, the police walked in and told Bon that the band was too loud. Of course, Bon was already a veteran at thumbing his nose at authority. 'So I gave them a gentle rubbish from the stage,' he later explained. 'I told the audience that the reason we were playing at RSL volume was that the "whatnots"—that's the word I used—don't like our usual volume.'

I wasn't there, but I can confidently say that Bon would have used a word slightly stronger than 'whatnots'!

Bon was searched in the car park after the show and told to leave town and never come back. Bruce Howe said it was 'like something out of a bad western movie'.

Fraternity also played some big gigs, supporting international visitors Deep Purple, Free, Manfred Mann and Jerry Lee Lewis.

In August 1971, the band had its biggest triumph, winning the national final of the Hoadley's Battle of the Sounds, beating Sherbet and Jeff St John. After coming third with The Valentines in 1969, victory for Bon was sweet.

Go-Set described Fraternity as 'musically one of the best bands in Australia', calling their win 'one of the most popular decisions yet'.

'The screaming and hysteria of previous battles wasn't there, but this is in line with the trend developing in Australian audiences. The winners got reactions, but they were for ability, not image.'

First prize was a trip to Los Angeles and $2000. Bon was finally on his way to America—or so he thought.

After Fraternity won the Hoadley's competition, Molly Meldrum raved about the band in *Go-Set*. 'The smartest move this group ever made was to settle in Adelaide, away from all the hassles and egos of the Melbourne and Sydney scenes,' he wrote. 'Their revision period on their farm and their learning and understanding about each other has turned this group into a threatening power, not only in Australia but on an international level. Why on earth their recording company, Sweet Peach, hasn't negotiated for an English or American release of "Seasons of Change" is beyond me . . . I suppose it's going to be the old story of yet another Australian group going overseas without any preparation or advanced publicity.'

As usual, Molly was right on the money. Instead of going to the US, Fraternity headed for London. With the benefit of hindsight, it wasn't a smart move. Fraternity's bluesy rock, with some heavy country influences, didn't fit into the UK glam scene, which was dominated by acts such as T. Rex, Slade and Gary Glitter. As Vince wrote in *Go-Set*, 'Fraternity are into a trip of their own.' But I'm sure the Americans would have been better able to relate.

Ahead of their UK trip, Fraternity were busy finishing their second album, *Flaming Galah*, which included a song written by Bon called 'Welfare Boogie', about how he struggled to get a real job. It was released as a single, but it didn't chart. It was Fraternity's final single with Bon.

I'm not sure if Fraternity ever managed to capture their live vibe on record. After all, the band was more of a concept and a lifestyle—how do you capture that on a record? 'What we've virtually done is cut down on all the external influences which actually hinder you from the music itself,' Bon told 3AK's Gary Mac. Fraternity also struggled to settle on just one sound—something that AC/DC would nail. 'We're really into country rock at the moment,' Bon said in October 1971. 'But just a year ago, we were playing heavily arranged classical stuff . . . it's just changing all the time.'

Go-Set summed up Fraternity's year at the end of 1971: 'Lots of getting it together, not enough of anything else. Oh, yes, they won the Battle of the Sounds.' In the end-of-year Pop Poll, Fraternity came in at number twenty-one in the Best Australian Group section. Sherbet took the title.

Go-Set put Fraternity on the cover of its issue of 18 September 1971, and Vince continued to talk up the band. 'When you've become as close to a group of people as I have to Fraternity, it's hard to talk about the group without being biased,' Vince admitted.

He was convinced that this was the band that would break Bon worldwide, saying that Fraternity were not a 'here today, gone tomorrow' group. 'They're here for good,' Vince claimed. 'They'll be around in some form or another in ten years' time.

'These guys are setting themselves up for later in life. After all, we do get old one day.'

But America remained a pipedream. Asked in October 1971 about the planned US visit, Bruce Howe said: 'We're just not good enough yet . . . or should I say we are not as good as we want to be.'

Fraternity briefly became known as Fang during their UK sojourn, but the name change didn't even rate a mention in the Australian music press. With the band out of sight, they were also out of mind, failing to crack a mention in *Go-Set* in 1972 and 1973.

While the band was known as Fang, they did a gig with a British band named Geordie, who had a hit with a song called 'All Because Of You'. Bon was impressed by their lead singer, a guy named Brian Johnson. Brian later revealed he was battling a bout of appendicitis when Bon saw him in action.

'I went down on my side, kicking and going, "Ooh!", but I kept on singing,' Brian told the *New York Post* in 2011. 'Apparently, he told the boys when he joined AC/DC: "I saw this guy Brian Johnson sing, and he was great. He was on the floor, kicking and screaming—what an act!" Of course, it wasn't an act. I was really ill.'

Bruce Howe says 'a lot of learning went on in England', which is another way of saying that Fraternity was yet another Australian band who starved in London. But it was another crucial part of Bon's musical apprenticeship. 'Bon was actually quite a shy performer,' Bruce recalls. 'He learnt that if you were doing a TV performance, you had to look down the barrel of the camera. And live, you had to take over the whole stage. And when we came back to Australia, that's what he did.'

'Bon learnt the wink and the leer,' drummer John Freeman adds. 'He was good at it, and he was never afraid to take his shirt off.'

Aside from the musical tricks, Bon got a lot out of the Fraternity days, not least the fact that he met his wife, Irene, who had befriended Vince in Adelaide. Bon and Irene married in Adelaide on 24 January 1972. She was twenty-one; he was twenty-five. Bon wasn't ready to settle down, but he had entered a new phase in his life.

Bon came over from Adelaide to show off his new bike . . .
and because he was lonely!

In 1975, Melbourne rock paper Juke *asked Bon to list his favourite singers:*

Little Richard—'Raunchy rock'n'roll voice . . . the way he keeps it up all the time . . . yeah, he's one of my favourite singers.'
Al Jolson—'For his showmanship and professionalism.'
Kenneth McKellar—'I like Kenneth for the beautiful ballads he sings and the way he sings them.'
Fats Domino—'For his incredibility and for his laidback rock'n'roll approach.'

A nice day for a weed wedding

Gabby

The times were changing. The Valentines had broken up. Betty and I had left school. Darcy and the guys were a little lost: the band was over; what next? No one had anything planned.

A couple of girls, Sue and Tess, had moved from Perth to Melbourne. Sue got engaged to Wyn and moved into the band's Toorak Road flat, while Tess got a flat around the corner in Cromwell Road. My Mum allowed me to move in with Tess. It was my first time out of home, and it was quite an experience. When The Valentines broke up, the guys moved out of their flat—and most of them ended up with Tess and me. Darce also moved in, as we were now officially an item. Then Wyn broke up with Sue, and he also arrived at Cromwell Road. All up, we had thirteen people living at that two-bedroom flat, including Ted and Wyn, Bon, Betty and Ted's sister. It was a little crowded!

I was now working at the In Shoppe with Mary during the week, while still working at the pharmacy on Saturday mornings. We had a lot of fun at that flat—I have a picture of me giving Bon a facial. The pharmacy job was handy for two main reasons: I could get our photos developed for free, and I was able to deal with the scripts for the guys when their extra-curricular activities necessitated a dose of penicillin.

I was only eighteen, but I wanted to have a baby, and we also wanted to have a party, so Darce—who was twenty-three—and I decided to get married. Unfortunately, Bon was in the UK with Fraternity, so he couldn't come to the wedding. But Paddy Beach had just arrived from South Africa with the first load of Malawi dope, so we were all set for a party.

(Speaking of weddings, Mary's friend Sandy wanted to marry Paddy, but Mary said, 'Do you think that's a good idea? Do you really want to be known as Sandy Beach?')

Dawn Klingberg, my boss at the Clementine label at the In Shoppe, made my dress. She was a very generous woman and a wonderful designer. My dress was lace and it was lovely. Old-fashioned, but without a veil. Mary and I also knew an up-and-coming designer named Ray Brown, and we asked him to make a suit for Darce. I bought some beautiful French velvet from Myer . . . it was a real Carnaby Street look—and Darce hated it!

Back in 1972, you either got married at a church or a registry office. We opted for a church but, much to the disgust of my mother and grandmother, we didn't choose a Catholic church. Instead, we got married at the Unitarian Peace Church, opposite the Freemasons Hospital in East Melbourne. Our friend Michael Gudinski kindly offered to have the reception at his nightclub, Garrison, in High Street, Prahran. The club had opened in February 1971, with Billy Thorpe & The Aztecs the headlining act. The promoters said, 'Only the cultured, sophisticated pop enthusiasts need arrive—the rest won't appreciate what we have to offer.' Fortunately, we knew the owners!

Darce and Scrooge spent the day before the wedding rolling joints for the reception. I would have preferred him to spend his time working on the van, which doubled as our wedding car. Darce was doing up the van, but it wasn't quite finished. There was no passenger seat, so I drove to the wedding sitting on a wooden fruit box—in my wedding dress. The uncovered engine was part of the cabin. And there were no seatbelts; I had to hang on for dear life.

As Darce has said to me many times over the years: 'How many chicks get driven to their wedding in a transit van? You were lucky!'

Darce's love for that van was even acknowledged in Jim Keays' autobiography, *His Master's Voice*. 'Darcy, The Valentines' roadie, started what I term the battle of the vans,' The Masters Apprentices singer wrote. 'His pride and joy was a souped-up Ford Transit that he boasted was the fastest van in the land. Not wanting to be outdone, all the self-respecting roadies around town put major work into making their vans faster, safer, flashier and more efficient.'

Like Darce, Jim missed those pioneering days in the sixties. 'In the seventies and eighties, as trucks and road crews grew bigger and eventually became convoys of semi-trailers, I'd hark back to these early times at the birth of it all, and recall Darcy's wide grin, a joint in one hand, spanner in the other, as he got ready for another big night.'

And there's no bigger night than your wedding day!

By this stage, my oldest friend Betty had moved to Adelaide and, unfortunately, had acquired a heroin habit and was in no shape to attend the wedding. Betty was a very proud girl and would not have wanted me to see her at a low point in her life. So I asked Tess to be my bridesmaid. Tess was engaged to an English boy, who came to Melbourne for the wedding, and stayed with us. He was a medical student, but I don't think he ever became a doctor. His life was never the same after our wedding. He had his first joint with Darce and he loved it. Suddenly, a mild-mannered, conservative Englishman was wearing a Hamburglar hat and a T-shirt covered in stars.

We were married on a Friday, and it was a rather informal affair. My younger brother, Mark—he was just sixteen—gave me away. My mother hired his suit, and with his little glasses, he looked like Mr Peabody. He was fine until someone gave him a joint—Darce and Scrooge's pockets had been full of them, which they threw into the air like confetti at the reception—then he was chewing bubblegum, blowing big bubbles. 'Are you okay, mate?' Darce kept asking him. But Mark just kept smiling and blowing bubbles, saying nothing.

My Mum later told me that my brother-in-law Graham was appalled by the proceedings and wanted to call the cops. 'Don't be stupid,' she told him. My mother was a progressive woman. Darce fondly remembers pulling into a service station after a gig, about three in the morning. He saw my Mum pull up in her blue Corolla with three drag queens in the back. For extra money, Mum used to choreograph for Les Girls. She always reminded Darce of Zsa Zsa Gabor. Mum later had a small part in the Lindy Chamberlain movie *Evil Angels*, playing an Indigenous woman—the director Fred Schepisi said she was the only Aboriginal woman he'd seen with pink hair.

Even though I was still a teenager, Mum was comfortable with my relationship with Darce. She figured I was going to do it anyway, so it was better for her to be involved so she knew what was going on. Which is a pretty good philosophy, I reckon. She's now in her late eighties and she still thanks Darce for looking after me.

After the reception, we stayed the night at the Travelodge and went home the following day. Life went on. I was pregnant by Christmas.

We kept in contact with Bon—wherever he was, he would write a letter outlining what he was doing. Communication wasn't easy in those days. There were no mobile phones and you were lucky if you had a landline at your house. And, of course, there was no Google or internet; we had to rely on letters or articles in the pop press to find out what Bon was up to.

On one memorable weekend during his Fraternity days, Bon rode his new motorbike from Adelaide to Melbourne, just to see us and to show off his new bike. He didn't have any of the biker gear; he was wearing just shorts and a singlet. He slept on the side of the road and woke up sunburned, wet and bitten by bull ants.

When Bon came to our house, he never knocked on the front door. For some reason, he'd always come to our bedroom window. Whenever we heard a *tap, tap, tap*, we knew it was Bon. He was always up for a chat, a cuppa and a smoke—usually it was late at night, after a gig. And Bon always kept in touch, no matter what he was doing.

In 1975, Darce was on the road with Wyn, who had moved into sound engineering after the end of The Valentines. The tour coincided with the birth of Wyn and his wife Sharon's second child, Emma, so Wyn missed the birth. With no mobile phones or emails, it took a while to let Wyn know that he was a dad for the second time, and he didn't meet Emma until two weeks later, when the tour finished.

Worried that Sharon would be all alone, I went to visit her in the maternity ward. On the way, I caught the tram to the AC/DC house at Lansdowne Road in East St Kilda to tell Bon the news. 'Would you like to come?' I asked.

'Sure,' Bon replied.

Bon was wearing nothing but jeans held together by safety pins, and when we rocked up to the Royal Women's Hospital they wouldn't let us in because he didn't have shoes or a shirt. So, we had to go buy thongs and a T-shirt.

When we arrived, Sharon was sitting in bed with baby boobs, and, of course, Bon couldn't stop himself from staring. She told the story at Emma's fortieth birthday: 'My daughter had just been born, her dad was on tour, and Bon Scott was staring at my boobs.'

When our daughter, Bec, was a baby, there was no such thing as organised mothers' groups, but a few people we knew were having babies, and one couple invited me over for a 'play date'. Their house was just around the corner from where Bon was then living with AC/DC. When I arrived, the kids started playing, and the parents made me a cup of tea. *This is nice*, I thought. Then they started shooting up. A lot of people in Melbourne developed heroin habits in the mid-seventies. It was not a good trend. I had no interest in hard drugs and I didn't want my baby daughter to be in such an environment, so I bundled Bec into her pram and quickly exited.

I was really shaken up. I didn't know what to do or where to go, so I went to the AC/DC house in Lansdowne Road. This was a notorious address, a so-called den of iniquity. But Bon welcomed me with a warm hug and a cup of tea. I burst into tears when he opened the door, and I told him what had happened. 'It's okay,' he reassured me. 'Don't worry about it, you're safe now.'

Bon calmed me down and then borrowed someone's car to take me home. He took me inside and got me settled. Years after The Valentines broke up, the boys were still protecting me.

Gab and her brother Mark on her wedding day.
Mark would spend most of that day blowing bubbles thanks to a joint from Darce.
Note Darce's amazing wedding suit.

It ain't no stretch limo!
Gab on the way to her wedding, sitting on a fruit box with a cushion in Darce's van!

AC/DC did several gigs in 1975 with a young Adelaide band called The Keystone Angels. Bon and Malcolm Young helped the band get a deal with the Albert label, and they then changed their name to The Angels. Singer Doc Neeson fondly recalled watching AC/DC. 'I used to love something that Bon would do on stage: he would look at someone in the audience, stare them down and look really mean. It was like he was stirring for a fight. The person would start to look very afraid. Just at the last minute, when it was getting really uncomfortable, Bon would smile at the guy, as if to say, "Only kidding." It gave the show a real rock'n'roll edge.'

Life's a beach

Darce

One of the strangest tales I ever got wrapped up in involved the bloke who introduced me to Bon—our little mate Paddy Beach. Paddy had been with me from my very first 'dabblings' in a rock'n'roll lifestyle—he always enjoyed a laugh and a smoke and we'd been together since the days of Compulsion, before he got me the gig with The Valentines. In those days, Bon, Paddy and I were most likely to be hanging out together, looking for a bit of trouble to get into. It was the three of us who broke the golden rule of 'no pot smoking' after The Valentines got busted: we lasted about a day.

After The Valentines days finished, Paddy ended up in South Africa. He must have been having the same sort of fun over there because we would receive some very interesting packages from him.

Paddy was pretty much responsible for 'turning on' Sunbury in '72. A few days before the festival, he sent me a card that contained about a thousand 'microdots' of acid. These were tiny cubes; four of them would fit on the head of a match, but it was powerful stuff. You'd cut one cube in half with a razor blade, and you'd be tripping on the crumbs for the next twenty-four hours. Even though the acid was amazingly strong, you'd still wake up the next day with no side effects, and go again! I was handing out these little babies left, right and centre; everyone loved them. (Almost everyone: Gab took just one-quarter of one cube, and kept her eyes shut for three days—I think she was too scared to open them. It was her one and only trip.) It made for a very wired weekend at Sunbury. Still, I managed to fulfil all my duties for Healing Force, an underrated Aussie band that I was looking after at the time.

So how did Paddy end up in South Africa? Well, there was a band from Zimbabwe (Rhodesia, as it was called at the time) called Holy Black that spent a fair bit of time in Australia in 1969 and '70. Their drummer quit just before they came over and Paddy ended up on the stool—he was introduced to the band by Daryl Braithwaite from Sherbet. Holy Black used to play at the Bondi Lifesaver, and they always went over pretty well. On vocals they had a soulful-sounding chick, Una Valli, who was a hit with the visiting servicemen on R&R from Vietnam in Sydney. The band went on to a residency at the Whisky a Go Go in Kings Cross, which was known as the biggest club in the southern hemisphere at that point. When one of Holy Black's main guys, Nick Pickhard, decided he'd had enough and returned to South Africa, Paddy went along for the ride and they kept playing as Holy Black. Weirdly, the members who stayed in Australia also kept playing as Holy Black, so you had two bands with the same name at the same time in different countries!

To make it more confusing, Paddy was also going under another name—Shane Mahoney. Officially, it was because of 'work visa issues in Rhodesia', but the reality was much more interesting.

Paddy sent us a couple of joints in a card when Gab and I were living at Palm Court in St Kilda. I smoked half of one; it was pretty heavy shit. Soon after, Mike Browning and Michael Gudinski turned up on a Sunday afternoon looking for some smoke, or some 'racehorses' as we called them—joints that were thin and quick. Gudinski had just got his licence and bought himself a bright yellow E-Type Jag. It was a pretty crazy first car to have, especially because Gudinski wasn't particularly coordinated.

I took one of the joints Paddy had sent and broke it in two. They just looked at me. I said, 'Smoke this. If you think you need some more afterwards, just let me know.'

Browning ended up backed against a wall, drooling, while Gudinski just rolled around the floor giggling. They didn't need the second half.

Soon after, Paddy decided to send over some more of this stuff.

By then, Gab and I had moved from Palm Court to just around the corner in Inkerman Street, and Paddy had come up with the perfect plan. Or so he thought.

Actually, the plan was already off to a shaky start. Paddy was supposed to have sent the samples to Palm Court using a false name, but he'd used my real one. That was okay; we'd got away with it. He was then meant to send his next 'correspondence' to my Dad's place in Coburg. That was when Paddy's plan came unstuck. Paddy was a great man but not big on the finer details. He sent a second package to Palm Court addressed to me, but because we'd moved out, the landlord opened it. And we had a problem: the landlord hated me.

I'd had a blue with the landlord because he used to crawl under the deck and look up Gab's dress. The CIB were already involved in that—he said I'd threatened to kill him . . . but that's another story.

A letter from Paddy followed two days later: 'What did you think of the shit? How many pounds can we get rid of?'

Good one, Paddy.

I had no interest in being a drug dealer—the dope was for personal use, and to give to my mates.

Unfortunately, the landlord intercepted the letter and I very quickly received a visit from the boys in blue, wanting to charge me with conspiring to import. I was hauled off to spend the night in the watch-house, which sucked because it was Melbourne Show Eve. This meant that it was a public holiday the next day, so I was going to be stuck there.

Luckily, Michael Gudinski came down to the watch-house at two in the morning and bailed me out.

I ended up having four court appearances because they kept getting adjourned, and at one stage I ended up in Pentridge on remand.

I got the full works while they were holding me, including one of the worst haircuts of my life. I was third in line when a big dude with a crew cut mentioned that he didn't think he needed a haircut, because he'd just had it done for a court appearance. The officer king hit him, split his eye open and screamed, 'You'll get a fucking haircut when I say so!'

So, when it was my turn, I was like, 'Yep, haircut, no worries!'

The old prisoner doing the cutting apologised. 'Sorry, mate,' he said, 'I've got to do this,' as my rock'n'roll hairdo fell to the ground.

This time, Scrooge and Coxy came to bail me out. They arrived as the guards dumped an aluminium box full of stew in the middle of the cell, which was holding about ten blokes. I was thinking, *I can't eat this shit* just as Scrooge and Coxy arrived . . . and cracked up laughing as soon as they saw my hair.

As I was gathering my stuff, Coxy piped up, 'How much for the haircuts?'

'We can give you one if you want, mate.'

Jesus, Coxy, we're not out of here yet!

Before my first court appearance, Michael Gudinski had organised a solicitor named Solly to look after me. And Solly soon discovered that this case was heavier than any of us originally thought. The drug squad were annoyed that I wasn't cooperating, and they were even less impressed when they found out that I'd got myself a solicitor.

There was unbelievable corruption in the drug squad at the time. They kept telling me how much jail time I was going to do—four years, and a $4000 fine.

'But we can help . . . if you give us the right information.'

And they mentioned a figure of up to $50,000.

The police wanted me to set Paddy up. Their plan was to fly me to Adelaide to meet him outside the Adelaide Town Hall, where they would nab him.

I played along until I could get to court and their plan fell apart. I was never going to cooperate and see my mate put behind bars.

I finally got my day in court at Russell Street. I saw my name on the board and stood at the top of the stairs looking for my barrister, who had been organised by Solly—a guy named Maitland Lincoln.

As I waited, a couple of guys from the drug squad tried to mess with me, to make me miss my court appearance, but soon enough my barrister arrived and the cops disappeared.

'Are you Maitland Lincoln?' I said to the big guy standing in front of me.

'Yes.'

'I'm John D'Arcy . . .' And I tried to tell him my story as he went into the court.

The next thing I knew it was time to enter a plea. I'd forgotten that my lawyer had talked my charges down to a $600 fine—if I pleaded guilty—so when the question was asked, 'How do you plead?', I naturally piped up with, 'Not guilty, Your Honour.'

Everyone in the court groaned.

Maitland Lincoln grabbed me. 'What are you doing? You're meant to plead guilty!'

(I have to confess I was a little ripped at the time—I'd had a number before court, to calm my nerves.)

So, we had to go through the whole thing again, and this time I got it right.

About a month later . . . lo and behold, Paddy turned up.

There was a knock on the door about seven o'clock one night. Standing there was a guy with thick glasses, Harris

Tweed coat, grey college trousers, a briefcase and an obvious wig. I thought, *This is a very weird visit from the Mormons.* Then I twigged. 'Fuck, Paddy, get in here. Look at my fucking haircut; you wouldn't believe what you've put me through! You sent the parcel and everything together, to my name!'

'Fuck, sorry, man.'

Then Paddy took off his wig and opened his briefcase: inside sat 13 pounds of rare dope from Malawi.

He and an English roadie named Jules had taken a 3000-kilometre trip from Johannesburg to the little village of Malawi to get this stuff. The plants were nine-foot high and dripped with resin, nearly as thick as molasses. The old men of the village would make it into a cob, like cobs of hash but with specks of head through it. Only the old men were allowed to smoke it because it was so potent. It was like a magical thing to them.

We couldn't even break it up. I remember having to use a bread knife. I'd cut it into little bits and we'd sell it as 10–15-millimetre discs for about $50. You only needed one or two puffs and the buzz would last all day.

And Paddy had 13 pounds of it. Jesus.

He mentioned the trips he'd sent over just before Sunbury, the microdots.

'Oh yeah, they went down well, mate,' I smiled. 'Everyone liked them.'

'Did you get any money for them?'

'No, I thought you had just given them to me. I just gave them away.'

'You were supposed to sell 'em!'

'Oh, sorry, mate.'

He was cool. It kind of made up for his getting me thrown in jail.

On his second trip over, a few months later, Paddy brought Jules the roadie with him. They travelled from Africa to Fremantle by boat and had the whole thing worked out. Paddy would get off the boat at Fremantle with all the tourists, a heap of shit taped to his body in garbage bags. He would whip into town and buy an overnight bag, put the dope in the bag and then head to the Ansett depot and freight the bag to Melbourne. He'd do the same thing in Adelaide, leave another bag in Melbourne, and then get off at Sydney clean and fly back to Melbourne. Lastly, he would duck into the Ansett depot in Melbourne, pick up the bags, and they're done; everyone could relax for a few days. A good plan, well executed!

Paddy hung out in Melbourne for a couple of days and we got into a bit of hash. There was hash everywhere in the sixties and seventies, coming in from places like Morocco, Nepal, Afghanistan, Turkey and Pakistan. Customs just hadn't twigged to it, and technology hadn't caught up. Mind you, the local stuff we started to get from Queensland and Griffith, which the Italians were growing, was every bit as good.

The time came for Paddy to get back on the ship to go to Sydney and, as you do, he decided to take a little bit of hash for the trip. Unfortunately, they found the pipe in his bag at customs in Sydney and took him away. Jules was on the ship and saw what had happened to Paddy, so he jumped on a plane to Melbourne to find us, despite not knowing where we lived.

Scrooge and I were watching telly with Gab one evening and we were suddenly freaked out when we saw a face in the window. We flew out and tackled the bloke on the front lawn; it was Jules.

'Darce, thank God I found you. Paddy's been nailed.'

Jules had been going from place to place looking through windows all around the area!

A few days later, Paddy turned up. He'd made up a story about losing his passport and having to get a duplicate. And they couldn't hold onto him because they'd only found a pipe.

Eventually, Paddy and Jules went back to Africa, and we finally got some peace and quiet. Still, there was more to come.

Months later, Paddy came back on his third trip and did his usual run—Freo, Adelaide, Melbourne, etcetera. This time, though, in Melbourne he changed his plan and brought himself undone. Paddy usually hired a car once he'd got into town, but this time he picked up one on the pier. The guards doing routine checks at the pier gate noticed that his clothes were bulging.

Four days later, I got a letter—from Paddy, in Pentridge. I read that letter, looking nervously up and down the street. Correspondence from Paddy tended to bring trouble.

Scrooge and I got $1000 together and went to bail him out. What Paddy did next was pretty impressive, straight out of a movie.

First, he went to see customs, in his thick glasses and wig, to confirm that he was still in town, saying he was out on bail and looking for work. The next day, he whipped around to the cemetery on Hawthorn Road in Caulfield where, after a bit of looking, he found a fresh gravesite for a bloke about the same age. Then, it was off into town to get an extract-of-birth for the name on the headstone: Shane Mahoney. He used this to get a new passport, and we had him on a plane two days later.

I didn't have any further contact with Paddy for thirty years. He continued to live an amazing life, getting himself in and out of many predicaments.

He ended up with a song-writing credit on one of the longest-running number one songs in Africa. He married a model, and after some sort of dodgy episode, he had to flee to Germany with his wife—ending up with yet another identity. Paddy spent ten years in Germany as Philip Dwyer, producing music for La Toya Jackson as well as . . . this is the icing on the cake . . . Milli Vanilli.

Gab managed to track him down by checking through the bands he'd been involved with in Africa. We finally found out he was working with a little production company in Cape Town and one day we decided to get in touch. I called the company and they gave me his mobile number.

'Hello, Shane?'

'Yeah?' came the reply, a little apprehensively.

'It's Darcy, mate.'

There was a pause. 'From Australia?' he asked.

'Yes, mate.'

First, he cracked up. Then he wanted to know if the cops had ever caught up with us—and whether I'd done any time.

'Mate, they didn't tie anything in . . . we're all cruising.'

We kept in touch from that day on, emailing pretty much every day, and speaking via Skype a few times a week. On Skype, we'd blow a number together and reminisce about our crazy days. I'd hold up some buds and he'd hold up a bag and exclaim, 'Swaziland!' It was funny remembering when we were young, stupid and reckless. I'm not condoning our behaviour, but I have to point out that it was a different time. It was the days of the Vietnam War, a time when it truly was sex, drugs and rock'n'roll. The future was uncertain and just about everyone was experimenting. We had fun and no one got hurt.

Paddy told us that his mum once asked why he did such crazy things. He said he just wanted to buck the system. And that was Paddy. He wasn't out to get rich, he just wanted to have fun and see how far he could push things.

And we were still having fun. One memorable night we even had a computer hook-up with Bon's little brother, Graeme, who hadn't seen Paddy since The Valentines days.

In 2011, Paddy decided he was going to move back to Australia. He was going to live with us until he got himself sorted. He packed up his house in South Africa—and then the poor bugger went and had a heart attack and died.

I miss him every day.

Paddy was a great mate. He was in the first band I ever worked with and got me the gig with Bon and The Valentines. If not for Paddy, I wouldn't have met Bon. And I've never known two bigger characters. Put simply, they were larger than life.

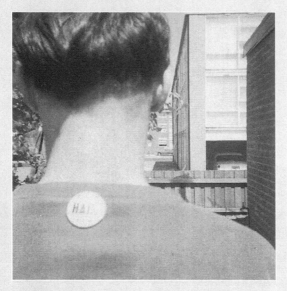

Darce's special hairstyle, courtesy of Pentridge Prison.

Back in Australia after Fraternity's unsuccessful sojourn in the UK, Bon hooked up with Adelaide musician Peter Head (also known as Peter Beagley, and the father of Australian actress and singer Loene Carmen). Peter was managing an art gallery when they met; Bon was doing some gardening jobs at the time.

'We'd have jam sessions,' Peter recalled in 2006, 'each with an old acoustic nylon-string guitar. Bon was basic on guitar, and only knew what we called the "cowboy" chords. But he had a good ear for what came when. I taught him chord progressions, scales and music theory, which he lapped up like a dog.'

Bon started singing with Peter's band, a loose collective named the Mount Lofty Rangers. Bon was also starting to write his own songs, including 'Clarissa', a country ballad about an Adelaide girl, and a tune called 'I've Been Up In The Hills Too Long'.

Peter spent $40 on a recording session, and Bon sang two songs written by Peter—'Round and Round' and 'Carey Gully'. The songs were released under Bon's name twenty-three years later, on a CD released by Head Office Records.

Bon enjoyed his time with the Mount Lofty Rangers, though in May 1974, after an argument at a band rehearsal, he stormed off on his motorbike and crashed into a car. He was in a coma for three days.

My bonny Scott

Mary

At the start of the seventies, I was moving away from rock'n'roll. I was no longer a teenager. Wyn was a lovely guy, but I was never going to marry him, so we broke up. Then The Valentines broke up, and I was getting serious about my work as a fashion designer. I also met a man named John Walton when we were both working for Norma Tullo. We hooked up at a party and pretty much moved in together the following week.

I got a job working for the very hip In Shoppe, opposite Myer, in Bourke Street in Melbourne, and I married John. But the marriage was over a couple of years later, though we stayed friends until John died of a brain haemorrhage.

And then Bon came back into my life.

I was working at the In Shoppe with a girl named Fi Zorzan. She'd come to Melbourne from Adelaide and we hit it off straightaway, but we never realised we had a mutual friend; that is, until the day Bon wandered into the In Shoppe.

'Mary!' he exclaimed. 'What are you doing here?'

'I work here,' I replied. 'What are *you* doing here?'

It turned out that Bon had come to visit Fi. He'd met her in Adelaide, but she'd spurned his advances. Bon—never one to take no for an answer—had ridden his motorbike to Melbourne to have another crack.

The three of us hung out for a couple of days and had fun. Fi confided that she liked Bon but didn't think he was husband material. And when it came to rock stars, she much preferred Barry Smith, the lead singer of The Town Criers.

Bon returned to Adelaide, and Fi eventually moved home, but she still resisted his charms. Bon responded by going out with Fi's little sister, Clarissa, which caused a massive sisterly fight.

I took a trip to Adelaide to visit Fi and catch up with Bon, and we all went to a big party in the Adelaide Hills at the Fraternity farm. That night Bon was in a bad mood and he decided to climb a big pine tree. Only problem was, he got stuck at the top and couldn't get down. It was quite a funny scene. I remember eating an icy pole, standing at the base of the tree and saying, 'Oh, look at Bon, I wonder how he's going to get down?'

It was typical Bon: doing something silly when he got angry. It took him hours to climb down and he was not happy.

Fortunately, Bon was usually the life of the party. One of my fondest memories is my friend Karin's twenty-first birthday. I didn't know what present to get her, so I gave her Bon for the night. When Karin opened her front door, I said, 'Happy birthday, here's your present'—pointing to Bon. She quickly unwrapped him, and both Bon and the birthday girl seemed very happy.

I saw Fraternity perform twice, in Melbourne and Adelaide. It wasn't really my cup of chai tea—it was a little serious—but it was obvious that Bon was developing musically and enjoying living in Adelaide.

When AC/DC started in Sydney, Bon was on his way back to Adelaide after Fraternity's ill-fated stay in London. AC/DC did their first gig on New Year's Eve in 1973 at Chequers, a club in Sydney. The line-up was singer Dave Evans, guitarists Malcolm and Angus Young, bass player Larry Van Kriedt and drummer Colin Burgess.

Just as AC/DC were starting out, British band Geordie, featuring Brian Johnson on vocals, toured Australia, spending nearly two months here at the start of 1974. Brian and the boys loved Australia; the only hitch came at the end of the tour when the band was refused entry to their farewell party. The manager of the Clock Hotel in Surry Hills said, 'Sorry, boys, you can't come in—long hair is banned.'

AC/DC made their first appearance in the pages of *Go-Set* on 15 June 1974. Mitch wrote the piece headed 'AC/DC: Sex And Energy Combined'.

Malcolm revealed that his older brother George's wife, Sandra, thought that 'AC/DC' was a good name for a group. 'If people want to think we're five camp guys, then that's okay by us,' Malcolm said.

The AC/DC line-up in mid-1974 was Malcolm and Angus, Dave Evans, drummer Peter Clack and bass player Rob Bailey. Malcolm believed that the band's youth was an advantage. He was twenty-one; Angus was nineteen.

'Most of the guys in Australian bands are getting on rather than getting it on,' he said, 'They don't relate to teenagers anymore.'

Dave explained AC/DC's approach: 'All we want to do is get the kids going.'

Go-Set said AC/DC was part of a 'new movement of working-class bands', including Hush, Finch, Sky, Fox and Ginger. '[They're] brash and arrogant, so confident they defy analysis. They challenge the oldies with the most powerful ammunition they can muster—sheer guts.'

Dave Evans was AC/DC's singer for ten months, during which time the band released its debut single, 'Can I Sit Next To You Girl', written by Malcolm and Angus.

I met Dave one night in South Melbourne. My friend Margaret Jackson (whom I would later introduce to Bon), knew Dave's girlfriend. He told Margaret about his band, AC/DC, revealing he was having some problems; the members were moving in different directions and he wasn't sure whether he wanted to stick around. Margaret and Dave's girlfriend convinced him to stay.

Then they sacked him.

Angus told a radio interviewer: 'Dave was more into the pop star side of things, more image than singing. We wanted somebody that had a great rock'n'roll life about them, and Bon was certainly the man for that.'

AC/DC met Bon through Vince Lovegrove in Adelaide when they were supporting Lou Reed in August 1974. Vince was running a booking agency. 'He said to us, "I've got a friend who'll drive you about,"' Angus would later recall. Up rocked a big, battered-up FJ Holden—with Bon behind the wheel. Angus and Malcolm remembered seeing Bon with The Valentines, and Angus had seen him on the telly playing drums with

Johnny Young's band, Kompany. 'One thing we knew—he couldn't drive.'

Initially, Bon suggested he could be the band's drummer, but the Youngs wanted a lead singer. After Adelaide, the band was embarking on Australian rock's toughest road trip—across the Nullarbor to Perth. Bon told them if they made it back to Adelaide, 'Look me up and I'll give you my answer.'

'We got back to Adelaide and he said he wanted to do it,' remembered Angus, who knew that Bon was the extra ingredient that AC/DC needed.

Dave and I are now Facebook friends, though I had to laugh when he posted a picture of himself wearing a ridiculous outfit, which made him look like an ice-skater. He compared it to Bon's leopard-skin vest and said something like, 'I think he even fancied the way I dressed and copied me.'

Give us a break, Dave!

You can't escape the fact that Dave was AC/DC's original lead singer, but Bon didn't copy any of his moves or his questionable fashion sense. Bon never copied anyone.

As AC/DC's then manager Michael Browning would later tell music writer Cameron Adams in the *Herald Sun*: 'No disrespect to Dave, but they wouldn't have made it with him as singer. He could sing okay, but he didn't have the character Bon brought into the band. The character, the sense of humour, the swagger. They were never going to go as far as they went with Dave out front. Bon was the real deal.'

The final issue of *Go-Set* hit the streets on 24 August 1974. Melbourne had to wait until May 1975 for a new weekly pop paper—*Juke*, which was started by Ed Nimmervoll (the Sydney music paper, *RAM*, also started in 1975). AC/DC were featured in *Juke*'s fourth issue, with Ed calling them 'new faces refusing to be ignored'. Bon reflected on his time with Fraternity: 'They worked on a different level to me. They were on the same level and it was way above my head.

'Fraternity didn't have a chance in England,' he added. 'This group has just got it.'

I could tell that Bon was happy to be in a simple, no-frills, straight-ahead rock'n'roll band. And he was enjoying renewing acquaintances with George Young, whom he met when The Valentines played with The Easybeats in Perth in 1967. 'He's like a brother—no, a father—to the group,' Bon said of George's involvement with AC/DC. 'He helps us with our writing. He doesn't tell us what to do, he just shows us how to get more out of the things we start.'

AC/DC's first *Juke* cover was the issue of 6 August 1975. Angus told Helen Barrett: 'My Dad likes what we do, but Mum, she thinks we're a bit rude. She saw us on the *Countdown* show when Bon was in a schoolgirl thing and lying on the floor, showing his all.'

After the party in the Adelaide Hills, I didn't see Bon for a long time. I was focusing on my career, and I heard he got married. Then one day, in late 1974, I ran into my good friend Christine. 'Guess what,' she said, 'Bon's in a band called AC/DC and they're playing at the Hard Rock!'

It was time to renew our friendship.

I left a message at the Hard Rock Cafe, a Melbourne venue, for Bon. He called me and I went to see the band play that night. I have to admit I was worried when I climbed the Hard Rock stairs. What if I hated the band? I knew I wouldn't be able to lie to Bon. Fortunately, I loved them; they were great.

Bon was finally in the band he'd dreamed of being in, one that was capable of conquering the world.

Bon came back to my house after the gig. I would have made him sleep on the couch; only problem was, I didn't have a couch, so I gave him some big cushions instead.

The following day, Bon returned to my place and informed me: 'I'm not sleeping on the floor tonight, Mary.' And that was the beginning of our love affair. It was passionate and intense.

I'd always been attracted to Bon, from the first day I met him.

I asked him about his marriage. He told me that Irene had tired of the rock'n'roll life—Fraternity's time in the UK had not been an enjoyable experience. Irene wanted a regular husband with a regular job, but Bon simply wasn't built to live that sort of life. 'I got a job in a factory,' he told me, 'but I walked in and said, "Fuck this," and I walked out again. I rang the guys in AC/DC and said I was in.'

We had a lot of fun. I had a big yellow brass bed, which used to bash against the wall. One night, Angus stayed in my spare room. The following day, Bon chuckled when he told me that Angus had said, 'Mate, what was going on in there? The walls were shaking, it felt like the house was going to fall down!' It was embarrassing, but I couldn't help but laugh. And I have to admit I had a wry smile when AC/DC's first post-Bon single was called 'You Shook Me All Night Long'.

Bon wasn't the best-looking guy in the world, and he could be quite uncouth, but he had a strange, indefinable essence and charisma. Women loved him. As AC/DC's bass player Mark Evans acknowledged, even his mum was in love with Bon.

I always called Bon 'Bonny', but he would freak out and plead with me not to say it in public, worried that his mates would pick up on it.

Of course, 'Bonny' was the nickname given to young Ronald Scott when he started school in Australia. His schoolmates were amused by his Scottish accent—he was the Bonny Scot.

All the guys at the Station Hotel, in Greville Street, Prahran—our favourite music venue at the time—started calling him Bonny. And because of my first name, he loved buying me Bloody Marys.

We always had music on at my place. Bon loved listening to Ike and Tina Turner records, and he loved a Scottish singer named Alex Harvey. He bought me an album by The Sensational Alex Harvey Band and it quickly became one of my favourites.

Bon would hang around my house while I went to work, though he'd often visit his old mate Jim Keays, from The Masters Apprentices. Bon was also active in the kitchen, though I can't say he was a culinary wizard. He liked to cook, even if it was just spaghetti—out of a can—on toast. I still smoked cigarettes back in those days, and I remember on one occasion when Bon went to light a cigarette for me at the gas stove and his hair started sizzling.

Bon's specialty was breakfast, and it was always ham and eggs. I don't think Bon liked bacon—it was always ham, never bacon. I also made sure that we had plenty of packets of Smarties, because Bon absolutely loved Smarties. Another thing Bon was fastidious about was his toiletries; he would carry his shaving kit and shampoo with him wherever he went.

To surprise Bon, I took him to see The Valentines' old guitarist, Wyn, and his wife, Sharon. Bon and Wyn enjoyed catching up, but Bon got upset when he remembered that Wyn and I had once dated. He was worried that he'd offended Wyn by rocking up to his place with his ex-girlfriend (he hadn't). Despite his wicked ways, Bon was always the gentleman.

Bon was nine years older than Angus, and seven years older than Malcolm, but despite the age difference, he got on well with the Young brothers. And Malcolm and Angus would often bring a leg of lamb over to my place and get me to cook it. They all loved a home-cooked meal.

Bon and Angus later cheekily did an interview with a music paper, in which Angus said: 'Bon gets the women with flats who cook him dinners.' Bon replied: 'I like to put my feet up. Not to mention other parts of my body.'

Hanging out with Malcolm and Angus suited Bon—three Scottish crazies all together. Malcolm was very serious at times, but he could also be very funny. Angus was just a kid. He rarely drank, but when he did, it was a disaster. I remember seeing a naked Angus swigging from a bottle of scotch one night when the band was living at the Freeway Gardens Motel in North Melbourne. I laughed and told him, 'Put your clothes back on, Angus!'

It was at this motel that Bon had the infamous sexual encounter with a Tasmanian woman named Rosie, whom he immortalised in 'Whole Lotta Rosie'. 'She was too big to say no to,' Bon told an American DJ in 1979. Bon estimated she was six feet tall and 120 kilos. 'So I had to do it . . . that was some mountain.' He also said Rosie had 'red curly hair and freckles and was very, very lusty'. AC/DC biographer Murray

Engleheart says legend has it that while Bon pretended to be asleep, he overhead Rosie doing sex sums with a friend. 'That's twenty-eight this week!' Rosie exclaimed.

I did not witness the encounter with Rosie, but Angus's girlfriend told me the sordid story.

Heather Johnson was living at the Lansdowne Road house when AC/DC moved to Melbourne. She worked in the kitchen at the Hard Rock Cafe, run by Bill Joseph and Michael Browning. Bill told Heather that it was the first time that Malcolm and Angus had lived out of home. 'If they come to the restaurant, give them anything they want,' Bill instructed. One day Heather was greeted by a young guy, peering over the counter, demanding a glass of milk. It was Angus.

That's how their relationship started.

Angus didn't spend much time at the Hard Rock's restaurant—he lived on Benson & Hedges Gold cigarettes, chocolate and cups of tea. And he spent most of his time in his room at the Lansdowne Road house, playing guitar.

But back to the Freeway Gardens Motel and the woman named Rosie, whom Bon would refer to as a 'Tasmanian Devil' on the *Live From The Atlantic Studios* disc, which turned up on the *Bonfire* box set. Heather came home from work; it was late and she was tired. She was heading for her room when she felt a hand on her shoulder. It was AC/DC's roadie, Pat Pickett. 'You may not want to go in there,' Pat informed her.

'What's going on?'

'It's all my fault,' Pat confessed. 'I set it up.'

Heather opened the door to the bedroom and was confronted by a naked and larger-than-life woman, who was lying on the bed, awaiting attention.

Bon and a few other degenerates were standing around, cheering each other on. Heather was surprised to discover how much the woman was enjoying the whole experience. Heather gave her a wave and left them to their party, hoping that it would soon be over because she wanted some sleep and Rosie was in her bed.

Pat Pickett tactfully justified the situation to Heather: 'The boys have never rooted a fat chick before.'

Pat thought it was time to tick that one off the list and he helpfully provided Rosie, who was a friend of his.

Heather had a chat to Rosie after all the shenanigans. 'She seemed like a really lovely girl,' Heather told me.

This was the seventies, when it really was sex, drugs and rock'n'roll. Men were doing their own thing, and women were too. The contraceptive pill had arrived and many women felt liberated. As John Watson would later write in the Australian edition of *Rolling Stone*: 'It was a time of that most dangerous rejoinder, "Why not?"'

AC/DC were certainly living like rock stars at the Freeway Gardens Motel. And, yes, sometimes it could be a tale of debauchery. But there was another side to the band as well. My friend Christine was a single mum, and when she had to go off to work at the Hard Rock, the 'wild rockers' would babysit her son, Jamie. Angus would share his milk and chocolate, and Bon would read him bedtime stories.

I had another experience with the band at yet another Melbourne motel—a much tamer experience than the Rosie extravaganza. Before moving to Lansdowne Road, AC/DC lived briefly at the Octagon Motel in South Yarra. Bon and I had a long lunch and we were rather drunk when we rocked up to the motel. It's the only time that the AC/DC boys were angry with me, because they had a gig that night. Bon had a remarkable ability to immediately straighten up, but I was smashed. Bon threw me in the shower and jumped in himself. He then put me in a taxi and sent me home.

Living in Melbourne helped shape AC/DC. Their then manager Michael Browning told Cameron Adams of the *Herald Sun*, 'I compare it to like when The Beatles were in Hamburg. It's where they found themselves as a group, it's where the character in the group came out. They were playing a lot of gigs, playing beer barns, where they were having stuff thrown at them. For any band to win those audiences over, you had to be pretty good. It was a formative period for them. If it hadn't been for Melbourne, AC/DC wouldn't have existed. There wasn't enough of a support system anywhere else in the country.'

Angus celebrated his twentieth birthday at the Lansdowne Road house. He got so drunk, he ended up out on the front lawn throwing up as we all laughed. Angus is definitely not a drinker.

Another night, Angus had an argument with Heather and she walked out. Malcolm tracked her down and begged her to 'come home'. Angus had gone berserk; he was drunk, smashing stuff and writing on the walls. The reason he was so upset? He was angry that Jimi Hendrix was dead (the American guitarist had checked out five years prior). Angus was cursing Jimi—if he was dead, they wouldn't be able to have a guitar-playing competition, to determine who was the best.

'They were great days,' Malcolm Young told radio interviewer Ed Nimmervoll. 'We were really like rock stars back then—the women and everything we were getting up to. They are our big memories. We'd been playing up to four gigs a day. That really shaped the band. As long as you could survive, it was better than doing a day job as a labourer. It was a mix of screw you, Jack, and having a good time and all being pretty tough guys. We just persisted. The training ground was Melbourne.'

At this stage, Bon, Malcolm and Angus were all working hard, writing songs for AC/DC's debut album. Bon loved a good time, but he also had a genuine work ethic. 'He would take a lot of time with his lyrics,' Angus explained in a radio interview. 'If someone asked him, he would say, "It's toilet poetry." But he wouldn't settle for second best. If he sang something and he felt it wasn't up to scratch, he'd be up all night till he was 100 per cent satisfied.'

Bon and the Youngs were fiercely ambitious. To them, AC/DC was the only band in the world and they were going to be number one. In the mid-seventies, Skyhooks were the biggest band in Australia and Bon resented their success, calling them Sky(fish)hooks or, if he was in a less complimentary mood, Cunthooks.

Bon rarely talked to me about the songs, though one day he came home and told me he'd written the lyrics for a new song called 'Love Song'. He insinuated that I was the inspiration. 'Love Song' is the softest song AC/DC ever recorded. It was a strange selection for the first single from the band's debut album, *High Voltage*, and radio preferred to play the B-side, the band's cover of 'Baby, Please Don't Go'. 'Love Song' is not loved by many AC/DC fans, but it's a special song to me.

Years later, a young woman came up to me at St Kilda's Prince of Wales Hotel. 'You're Mary, aren't you?' she asked.

The woman told me that she'd met AC/DC's former bass player, Mark Evans, in Sydney. She'd told Mark that 'Love Song' was her favourite, joking that, 'Bon wrote that for me.'

'No,' Mark replied. 'That song was written for a girl in Melbourne named Mary.'

Whenever Bon came to the In Shoppe to take me out to lunch, he was always barefoot, and we'd have to go to Coles to buy him a new pair of thongs. This process took ages because Bon would be stopped by fans wanting autographs. I never saw Bon refuse a fan's request. He was always friendly, with a big smile on his face when he signed a piece of paper or a piece of flesh. He loved it.

My physical relationship with Bon unravelled at the end of 1974. On New Year's Eve, I arranged to meet him at the Hard Rock Cafe. First, I had some drinks with my friend Toni and a roadie named John Brewster, who worked with Skyhooks. John had to visit his parents in Chelsea, so I tagged along and they promised to then drive me to the city. I stayed in the car while John caught up with his mum and dad, and, unfortunately, I fell asleep. Time got away from us and I never made it back to the Hard Rock in time to see Bon.

Of course, these were the days before mobile phones and I had no way of letting Bon know that I wasn't going to make it. Bon was apparently concerned about my whereabouts, running around, saying, 'Where's my girl? I've lost my girl!'

And then Judy King—younger sister of Betty King, the girl who introduced Gabby to The Valentines—turned up, and, suddenly, Bon had a new girl. That was Bon—he was never going to be without female company for very long.

I didn't see Bon until a couple of weeks later when I went to an AC/DC gig. He was living with the band at their house in Lansdowne Road, East St Kilda, but they didn't have a phone. Whenever Bon wanted to speak to me, he would have to go to a phone box, or just drop into the In Shoppe or my house.

When we caught up, we were both sorry. Bon told me about Judy. He had moved on, but we remained friends. We were always going to be close. I was also moving on, planning to move to London in April, after I'd finished designing that year's winter knitwear range.

I often rue not making it to the Hard Rock that New Year's Eve. Judy King was a beautiful girl, but this was not a great relationship for Bon. When Mr King found out that a rock singer was going out with his seventeen-year-old daughter, he flew into a blind rage. He warned Bon not to sleep with her. But Bon was frightened of no one and he continued seeing Judy. Her dad then decided to pay Bon a visit.

Number 6 Lansdowne Road became a notorious rock'n'roll address, a contender for music's 'vilest den of depravity', according to UK magazine *Mojo*. But I visited the house many times and I think its infamy is overblown, though Bon played up the location's lascivious reputation when he told the UK press: 'We used to have this house in Melbourne and we all used to live there and all these chicks used to come around. They were all dropping mandies [Mandrax] or whatever and we didn't mind 'cause we were getting a screw.'

Bon's confrontation with Mr King was the ugliest incident at the house. It ended up in *The Truth* newspaper, in a piece by

Dave Dawson, headed: 'Pop Star, Brunette And A Bed: Then Her Dad Turned Up!'

'She is seventeen and capable of making up her own mind,' Bon told Dave.

'I had returned from Sydney the night before and she was there waiting for me. We were making love when our roadie, Ralph, knocked on my bedroom door and said someone wanted to see me urgently. I told him to come back in two hours because I was busy.'

Eventually, Bon, wearing only shorts, went to the door, where he was greeted by Judy's dad. 'I can see you've got your fighting shorts on,' Mr King said. According to Bon, Mr King took out his false teeth and challenged him to a punch-up.

Mr King beat Bon up out the front of the house, knocking him into a rose bush. With his teeth knocked out, Bon called it 'the worst beating I have ever had . . . The girl's father has never given her any love and he certainly showed me none'.

Angus later recounted his version of the incident to UK magazine *Sounds*: 'I remember Bon was caught once with a brunette bird . . . he was in this big double bed when the roadie knocks on the door and shouts, "Bon," and he's sticking it up this young bird. Anyway, the roadie keeps yelling, "Bon," and he says, "Go away, I'm having a . . ." and in bursts this chick's old man.'

I didn't know Judy well. All I knew was she was Betty's little sister, she was gorgeous and she had a pet parrot that liked to screech swear words. Sadly, Judy also had a bad drug problem. Judy and Betty dared Bon to have a hit of heroin. Never one to resist a dare, Bon stupidly agreed. Having no tolerance to the drug, he immediately passed out. To try to revive him, they shot him up with some speed. Bon ended up in hospital.

I was living in London when I heard the news. I wrote Bon a letter, which basically asked him what the fuck he was doing.

I had a lot of fun in the UK, spending some time hanging out with the band Slade, who I met because my friend Margot was going out with one of their team. I remember telling one of their roadies about AC/DC. 'AC/DC?' he said with a bemused look on his face. 'You know that means bisexual?' I immediately wrote to Bon to tell him, but Bon didn't seem to mind. In fact, I think he liked the sexual ambiguity of the band name.

In fact, he once gave a now-famous answer when he was asked whether he was AC or DC: 'Neither. I'm the lightning flash in the middle.'

After telling Bon about the bisexual connotation of AC/DC's name, I joked, 'Next thing you'll be on the telly dressed as a girl.' And that's exactly what Bon did, appearing in a school girl's uniform—complete with long blonde pigtails and tattoos—when the band performed 'Baby, Please Don't Go' on *Countdown*.

Bon was drawn to interesting people. He didn't care if you were rich or poor, gay or straight, he simply enjoyed the company of interesting, genuine people. He loved a friend of mine named Lynnie, who worked in the menswear department at the In Shoppe (taking over from Derek Pellicci, who became the drummer in the Little River Band). Bon loved Lynnie because she was a character. She would wear a big fur coat and be naked underneath. She had a Chihuahua with pierced ears, and she was always accompanied by her pet rabbit.

Lynnie and Bon kept trying to out-shock each other. When Lynnie was at my place, she would open the door to Bon, totally nude. She had a big panther tattoo on her upper thigh, but Bon would pretend this was nothing unusual. 'Hi, Lynnie,' he'd casually remark as he walked down the hall. And in a letter, Bon cheekily asked me to pass on a message to Lynnie: 'Tell her I've had a panther tattooed in the same place and does she want to mate them?' Bon knew that Lynnie wasn't interested—she was a lesbian.

One night, Lynnie dropped her pants on stage at an AC/DC show. Bon responded by dropping his false teeth in her chocolate sundae. Bon had false teeth as a result of his motorbike accident in Adelaide. Sadly, Lynnie met an unfortunate end. She had drug debts and was found dead, presumed murdered.

There's no doubt that Bon and Judy King were not good for each other. Fortunately, AC/DC was Bon's top priority, and he went overseas with the band. *Juke* announced the band's departure in its issue of 27 March 1976, saying 'they go with hopes high' before giving the band a bit of a backhander: 'You've all heard worse music . . . When one considers how big were bands like Slade and T. Rex, one must admit that indeed anything could happen.' The paper knew that Bon deserved success. 'The most pleasing aspect of the whole thing is seeing Bon Scott really doing it. Anyone who sticks to music as long as Bon has deserves a decent reward for guts alone.'

Molly Meldrum did a farewell interview with the band at Sydney Airport. 'What do you think you owe your success to?' Molly asked.

'It's nothing to do with us at all,' Bon replied. 'Our success is due to the taste of the public.'

Just before AC/DC embarked on their UK adventure, they made a film clip for 'It's A Long Way To The Top (If You Wanna Rock'n'roll)'. Made with the crew from *Countdown*, it was a simple concept: the band playing on the back of a flatbed truck travelling down Swanston Street in the middle of Melbourne. The budget was just $380, but the result was classic, probably the greatest Australian music video of all time. It showcases Melbourne as it was in the mid-seventies, and the clip has been viewed millions of times on YouTube.

When the band left for the UK, Bon told journalist Susan Joy: 'You know, we're not really leaving . . . I mean, it's just like going to the toilet, except you're away a little longer.' But I got the feeling that it would be a while before I would see my friend again.

Unfortunately, in London Bon reconnected with an old acquaintance from Adelaide, Margaret Smith, who was now known as Silver Smith. Silver was active in the UK music scene—Bon told me she had partied with Keith Richards. She also gave Bon her opinion of AC/DC, saying they would fail if they didn't become a punk band. But AC/DC never wanted to be seen as punk. Not long after *Highway To Hell* was released, American journalist Steven Rosen asked: 'How do you feel about punk bands? Any sympathy for them?'

'None,' Angus replied, as Bon added, 'What's a punk band?'

In 1977, AC/DC played at New York's CBGB's. The punk patrons greeted the band's blistering performance with silence. Malcolm Young says the band learned a valuable lesson that night: 'You play shitass, the kids go wild. Play great, and everybody sits there.'

Bon was never a punk and he was never a big drug user. Sure, he was up for anything, but he was a drinker, not a drug-taker. If it was there, he'd have it, but Bon would never go out of his way to score drugs. Yes, I saw drug use, but I never saw drug abuse. The only strange experience I had with Bon was the night he came to my place a little out of it. He must have taken an early version of ecstasy because he was very lovey-dovey and kept wanting to suck my toes. 'What the fuck are you on?' I said as he put my foot in his mouth. We had a great night.

I was amused when, later, Bon's ex-wife Irene told me of her first encounter with Bon, at a party in Adelaide. Looking for the toilet, Irene mistakenly walked into a bedroom where a naked Bon had his lips wrapped around a young girl's foot. 'I couldn't get the image of that girl's foot out of my head,' Irene said.

Soon after, Irene saw Fraternity live and was struck by Bon's tight jeans. Looking at his crotch, she remarked, 'What a well-packed lunch.'

'Yeah,' Bon replied, 'two boiled eggs and a sausage.'

Bon was a funny fucker. And I could see why he loved Irene—they shared a wicked sense of humour.

When we got to know each other, after Irene and Bon had broken up, Irene would often introduce me to people: 'This is my husband's mistress.'

Irene is a great girl, and we quickly became friends after she moved to Melbourne from Adelaide at the start of 1976. I remember I was having drinks with friends at home when there was a knock on the door.

'Hi, I'm Irene,' the striking blonde woman said, standing on my doorstep with Vince Lovegrove's sister, Sue. 'I'm Bon's wife.'

Bon—who was splitting his time between Melbourne and Sydney, where AC/DC were recording the *Dirty Deeds Done Dirt Cheap* album—had given Irene my address and phone number and instructed her to look me up in Melbourne. We had a lot to talk about. She told me about Bon's Fraternity days; I told her about his time in The Valentines. Irene says, 'It was nice to speak to someone who liked Bon as much as I did and knew him as something more than just a singer in a band.'

Though Irene and I are great friends, I have never talked about the fact that I was Bon's inspiration to write 'Love Song'. The name Mary appeared in another AC/DC song, the charmingly titled 'Go Down', the opening track on the *Let There Be Rock* album. Bon declares his love for a woman named Mary in the song. Apparently, when she heard the song, Irene quizzed Bon: 'Who's this Mary? Is that a good moll's name?'

Thanks for that, Irene!

I liked Irene so much, we shared a house in Carlton, near the venue Martini's, where we saw a lot of great bands. I was living with Irene when her divorce from Bon became official, in March 1977. I arrived home to find her drinking a bottle of wine on her own. 'Divorce party,' she smiled.

I don't think Irene was happy that Bon gave me his wedding ring. He and Malcolm Young dropped into the In Shoppe one day to take me out to lunch. We went to the Bombay Bicycle Club, where, totally unexpectedly, Bon took the ring off his finger and said, 'This is for you.'

'Oh, thank you,' I mumbled. I was a little shocked and didn't know what to say. Malcolm just smiled—the AC/DC guys had often jokingly referred to us as 'Mr and Mrs Scott'.

I wear Bon's ring every day.

Strangely, Irene later gave me her wedding ring when we had lunch at the same venue. 'Here,' she snapped, 'you've got Bon's, you might as well have mine!'

I kept Irene's ring safe until she wanted it back.

AC/DC were signed to Atlantic Records by Phil Carson in the label's London office. AC/DC's first UK tour, in 1976, was billed as the 'Lock Up Your Daughters' tour, which Rolling Stone *would later say was in honour of 'Bon's animal sexuality'.*

The American edition of Rolling Stone *savaged the US release of* High Voltage *in December 1976, saying the hard rock genre 'has unquestionably hit its all-time low'.*

Reviewer Billy Altman took aim at Bon, stating that he 'spits out his vocals with a truly annoying aggression which, I suppose, is the only way to do it when all you seem to care about is being a star so that you can get laid every night'. He concluded: 'Stupidity bothers me. Calculated stupidity offends me.'

Living the dream

Darce

The first time I saw Bon singing with AC/DC was at a gig in Sydney at the end of 1974. Bon was wearing bright satin overalls with a little bib'n'brace. He had nothing on underneath and his balls were hanging out. It wasn't a great look, but I knew that musically he'd found his home. I thought Fraternity was a good band, but this was a *great* band.

I was buzzing when I caught up with Bon after the show. 'Fuck, mate, that's the best I've seen you fire up.'

'Yeah,' Bon replied, 'I've got these young dudes behind me, kicking me in the arse, and I feel great.'

'Not too sure about the pink overalls, though,' I laughed.

It was great seeing Bon front a no-frills rock'n'roll band. He was reborn. Just a microphone in hand, backed by some killer riffs.

By this time, I was doing some pretty big gigs, too, working for the promoter Paul Dainty on tours such as Leo Sayer, Bad Company and Joe Cocker. We were doing big shows all over the country, but it was the same old story—setting up, packing up, driving, not getting much sleep. At least we were staying at better hotels, so the food was good. But we didn't care how far we had to drive, as long as the gig was good.

Bon stayed with us in Brighton when he came to Melbourne with AC/DC at the end of 1974, and he brought drummer Phil Rudd with him. Phil slept in the dining room; Bon had a room out the back.

On another trip, we saw AC/DC at Festival Hall, which was a big gig for the band. Bon had organised the tickets and we were about four rows from the front, smack in the middle. We were probably the oldest people in the crowd—I was twenty-five and Gab was twenty—and everyone else was going absolutely nuts. I remember Bon was singing when he spotted us. 'Come on, Darce,' he yelled. 'Get into it!'

Gab and I were so grown up we even had a Holden station wagon. After one AC/DC gig, we took Bon, Malcolm and Angus out for a night on the town. We drove to the Chevron on St Kilda Road, with Angus eating a Mars Bar and drinking a milkshake in the back seat. Angus seemingly lived on milk and chocolate bars. Unfortunately, our friend Nicky Pappas wasn't on the door that night and the bouncer wouldn't let us in because Angus and Malcolm were too young and Gab was wearing sneakers. I was the only one who would have been permitted to enter because I was wearing a lovely pair of corduroy pants.

So, we took the guys back to their hotel, the Chateau Commodore on Lonsdale Street. That was our big night out!

All the hard yards Bon put in during his Valentines days paid off in AC/DC. He was match-fit. He outlined AC/DC's punishing schedule in an interview in 1979: 'We would play our first gig at lunchtime in a school. After that, we'd bring our gear to a nearby pub to play two sets in the afternoon, and finish off by doing two sets at another club. That was the price to pay.'

It was The Valentines days all over again. Except this time, Bon didn't have to share the vocal duties. He was front and centre, and you could tell he was playing the music he truly loved.

Things happened quickly for Bon and AC/DC. Bon did four years with The Valentines and they never released an album; four months after he joined AC/DC, they released their debut album, *High Voltage*. Gab and I were living at Monbulk then, which was about an hour out of town, but Bon and his brother, Graeme, came to see us. Bon wanted to personally give us a copy of the album. He was so proud.

Soon after AC/DC released *High Voltage*, they got a new bass player—Melbourne's Mark Evans. Bon wasn't at Mark's audition. In fact, he didn't meet Mark until five minutes before his first gig with the band, at the Waltzing Matilda Hotel in Springvale, but they became great mates. And Mark had a lovely description of Bon: 'What a character that guy was. By his own admission, he was a great bunch of guys.'

Mark also tells a wicked story about a bender with Bon in Paris. Surveying the scene from the tiny balcony at their hotel, Mark remarked, 'How good is this?' When Bon didn't answer, Mark inquired, 'Are you okay, mate?' Bon was staring into the distance. 'There's a tower just like that in Paris,' he informed Mark, pointing at the Eiffel Tower. Mark decided it was time they got some sleep.

Just ten months after their debut, AC/DC released their second album, *T.N.T.*, featuring Bon's classic 'It's A Long Way To The Top (If You Wanna Rock'n'roll)'. And the band's manager, Michael Browning—the man who brought Compulsion to Melbourne—had organised an international deal.

AC/DC might not have become AC/DC if not for Michael Browning. He was a believer. And Michael's venues— Bertie's, where he booked the bands, and Sebastian's, which he co-owned—were instrumental in the development of Melbourne's music scene. He could have written a book just on Sebastian's. We had so many great times there. I particularly remember the night Barry Humphries turned up dressed like the Hamburglar: he walked up the stairs and surveyed the scene, then hissed, 'Fucking peasants,' and walked out.

In 1975, Bon invited Gab and me to a gig AC/DC were doing at Melbourne's Hard Rock Cafe, which was at the site of the old Bertie's, on the corner of Spring and Flinders streets. Bon greeted us when we arrived, and beamed as he hugged me.

'Mate, we're doing it,' he grinned. 'We're going to England. I want you to come.'

'What?' I wasn't sure if I'd heard right.

'We're going to England, mate. I want you to come with me.'

This was what we'd both dreamed of. All those nights spent smoking at that little Toorak Road flat, talking about how we wanted to take an Aussie band overseas and kick arse.

I didn't know whether to laugh or cry.

I understood where Bon was coming from. He knew it was a long way to the top and touring overseas wouldn't be easy. He dug his new band mates, but he was also aware that he came from an almost different generation, as he was so much older than Malcolm and Angus. Bon wanted to have a mate with him; someone who knew him and someone he trusted.

Bon was growing into the rock star we always knew he would become, and that can be a dangerous time. When you're famous, everyone wants to know you. But are they your friends just because of your fame? Bon and I were mates when he had nothing but his talent and his street smarts. We'd slept in vans together. I knew how he functioned. I could read him on stage. A good roadie can watch a band and know what they need, often even before they know.

'So, can you come with me?' Bon asked.

So many things were rushing through my head. I loved Bon and I knew how much fun we would have on the road. But then I looked at Gab and thought about how much I loved her and our baby daughter, Bec. Having come from a broken home myself, I didn't want to see my own kid deal with all of that. And I knew that if I went with Bon and AC/DC, I might never come back.

'Mate,' I said, my voice quivering, 'I can't . . . I can't go. I'm sorry, mate.'

Bon looked at Gab and he understood. He used to call Gab and me 'Ma and Pa Kettle', and while I thought he was living the dream, I think he thought Gab and I were living the dream.

After telling Bon my decision, he had to go on stage. We both had tears in our eyes, but the show must always go on.

Michael Browning spotted me as I walked away. 'Hey, mate,' he smiled. 'Come into the office.'

I followed him, and found Bill Joseph, The Valentines' old manager, also there.

'Bon wants you to come overseas with us,' Michael said.

He was surprised that I didn't look happy.

'I know,' I replied. 'I've just told him I can't go.'

Michael and Bill could see how disappointed I was. They also knew there was nothing they could say that would change my mind.

To go on the road and look after Bon, or stay home and look after my family: my mate, or my wife and daughter? It was a horrible dilemma.

And I've thought about it every day since.

Meeting up with AC/DC on the road between Melbourne and Sydney.

Darce: 'I was touring with Black Sabbath at the time. This is Bon, overalls down and fingers up his nose, with one of the crew, and me in the big Paul Dainty truck, exposing myself.'

Darce on tour with Black Sabbath. The Paul Dainty crew, left to right—
lighting man Peter Wilson, Darce and sound engineer Russ Kidner.

Atlantic Records boss Ahmet Ertegun met AC/DC for the first time after they played at CBGB's in New York. 'They were cocky little kids,' Ertegun later recalled. 'They kinda put me through the ropes. They didn't have any respect for older people.' Backstage, Ertegun thought the band was laughing at him, but he turned around to see Bon peeing into an empty beer can.

Australian record producer Mark Opitz engineered AC/DC's Powerage *album. He enjoyed the experience. 'AC/DC are the sort of guys that get all their aggression out on stage. In real life, they're just nice guys, no ego. They did a lot of charity work, even back then. Far from the devil worshippers they were meant to be, they were probably the nicest bunch of people I've ever worked with. Bon was a sweetheart. He took his lyric writing very seriously but always left it to the last minute and he'd have all this stuff on bits of scrap paper. I remember one night we were leaving the studio and Bon came up to me and said, "Mark, have you got anything to smoke?" And I had a little bit of hash, about an inch-and-a-half long in my pocket. So, I broke it in half and said, "There you go." He said, "Thanks, mate, I won't forget this."*

'About six months later, I'm walking down a corridor at Alberts, eating a pie, and there's Bon going, "Mark, Mark, I've been looking for you for a couple of days. I just wanted to give you this." And he pulled out a massive block of hash, the size of a block of chocolate. He breaks off half and gives it to me. I gave him half, so he gave me half.'

A giant dose of rock'n'roll

Mary

'Lock up your daughters and keep tabs on your sons, 'cause the future teen kings of rock'n'roll are coming your way!' So declared UK music magazine *Sounds* soon after AC/DC arrived in London in 1976.

England didn't exactly embrace AC/DC with open arms, but along with the music press's usual lame Aussie references—'I wallaby your man' and 'More chunder from Down Under'—the band quickly found some serious supporters in the UK media.

'We're putting our money on top Australian band AC/DC,' *Sounds* stated.

Caroline Coon raved about 'It's A Long Way To The Top (If You Wanna Rock'n'roll)' in *Melody Maker*: 'It's up there with Kiss and Angel, but if m'ears don't deceive me, they have an added plus by being able to play the bagpipes. Mind-boggling.' And then, almost as an afterthought, she added: 'They're Australian.'

Unfortunately, AC/DC's first UK tour got off to a bumpy—or false—start. They were meant to go on the road with Back Street

Crawler, the band belonging to Free guitarist Paul Kossoff, but just before the tour, Kossoff died of a drug overdose, aged just twenty-five. Bon responded sensitively in the pages of *RAM*: 'That cunt Paul Kossoff fucked up our first tour. Wait'll Angus gets hold of him.'

It was a setback, but nothing was going to stop AC/DC's international assault.

Sounds summed up AC/DC's first international album, *High Voltage* (a combination of the band's first two Australian albums, *High Voltage* and *T.N.T.*): 'Very facile, but nonetheless quite endearing with a definite slant towards the inelegant/ obscene.'

Back home, we lapped up news of the band making inroads internationally. Many Australian acts had tried to break into the overseas market and most had failed. As AC/DC went to the UK, their arch rivals, Skyhooks, went to America, where their manager, Michael Gudinski, had trumpeted news of a AUD$1.5 million deal.

Legendary Melbourne DJ Stan 'The Man' Rofe made this prediction: 'Out of Skyhooks and AC/DC, two of the groups presently overseas, I think that possibly AC/DC have the greater chance of succeeding. They are a raunchy little punk rock'n'roll band and, in their own way, they are excellent, but they are still very much teenybopper orientated.'

In reality, Skyhooks saw none of the money from their overseas deal, which was based on the band delivering an unrealistic ten albums over five years. They ended up releasing just two albums in the US—*Ego Is Not A Dirty Word* and their third album, *Straight In A Gay Gay World* (which was retitled *Living In The 70's* for the American market). Many Americans saw Skyhooks as a pale imitation of Kiss—a group the Hooks were unaware of until they actually went to America. Jack Lloyd's review in the *Philadelphia Inquirer* was typical of the US response to the Skyhooks tour: 'The grand pop music industry tradition of super hype has taken a severe setback with the arrival of Skyhooks, currently on its debut tour of America in the wake of shameless proclamations about this being the hottest group to ever come out of Australia.

'Well, if Skyhooks (which appeared as the opening act for Uriah Heep at the Tower Theatre Monday night) is the kind of act that can be considered a sensation in Australia, there is little wonder why so few acts break beyond the Down Under confines to become international hits.

'Skyhooks, to be blunt, is without a single redeeming quality.' Ouch.

AC/DC had a point to prove. They weren't the biggest band in Australia, far from it. When AC/DC appeared on the cover of *Sounds* in 1976, the UK magazine asked, 'Are Schoolboys The Future of Rock'n'roll?' They also asked Angus if AC/DC was the biggest band in Australia. He lied—or certainly stretched the truth—by claiming, 'I'd say we are. There are three or four top bands back home, Skyhooks and Hush among them, but each tends to cater for a certain audience. We're the only band that's able to cover the whole spectrum.' I knew that for Angus and Bon—and all the AC/DC boys—there was only one band in the world: AC/DC. They just had to prove it.

Skyhooks guitarist Red Symons admits that the Hooks didn't have the same hunger. 'When we did our third album, we had an American engineer, Bill Halverson, who'd also worked with Crosby, Stills & Nash,' Red recalls. 'He said to us, "You guys have been successful in Australia, but you guys don't realise what it would be like to be successful in America." And I thought, "You're fucking wrong, you are so wrong," because these things are all relative. Australia is no backwater, and we were as successful as it's possible to be. Girls cried when they saw us. So, how was it going to be different in the US? It's going to be larger, but what differences? It's going to be the same. And, I guess, underpinning all that was the realisation—and we all felt the same but it was never articulated—that I honestly believe that none of us really wanted to succeed in America. We weren't hungry to succeed in America. We didn't care. It was just going to turn into the same job on a bigger scale.'

Contrast that attitude with AC/DC's approach. As Bon said in 1976, 'There ain't nothin' we won't take on. The moon? Right, we'll be there next week.'

Skyhooks did just one US tour. The balance sheet showed that they lost more than AUD$90,000.

AC/DC weren't an overnight success in the UK, but with every gig they won over new fans. During their first UK tour, they did several shows at London's legendary Marquee Club. It wasn't a massive venue, holding between 500 and 700 people, but it was filled with history, and after AC/DC played, the club's manager, Jack Barry, made a statement that helped build the AC/DC vibe: 'AC/DC are the most exciting thing I've seen at The Marquee since Led Zeppelin.'

An English reporter named Doug Crawford caught up with AC/DC in London in July 1976 to do an interview for *Countdown*. It was the middle of the day in James Street, Covent Garden, and Bon was wearing nothing except a pair of denim shorts. Strangely, the shorts had a belt. Even stranger was the fact that Bon had a banana tucked down his shorts. Doug must have been tempted to ask, 'Is that a banana in your pocket or are you just pleased to see me?' Instead, he mentioned The Beatles and The Rolling Stones, which prompted Bon to declare, 'We're better. Who needs them—they're last year's model.'

Despite the accolades, AC/DC didn't have any chart action in the UK in 1976. The biggest Australian story on the UK charts that year was Sherbet, who had a Top 5 hit with 'Howzat'. *Juke*'s Christie Eliezer challenged Angus when the guitarist said, 'Sherbet haven't got much happening over there . . . I didn't even know they were in the country, to tell you the truth.'

'You call getting a Top 5 single nothing?' Christie responded.

Bon shrugged his shoulders. 'You get so many bands on the charts that don't mean anything. Look at Hot Chocolate—they've had about six number ones there and our tour sold twice as much as theirs. There are singles bands and touring bands, and touring bands are the ones that last.'

Christie remembers that Bon thumped the table to make the point: 'Look, mate, the only band that's done anything in England is AC/DC. The rest of them are just bullshitting!'

Christie also asked Bon what the English groupies were like, and his reply revealed that Bon wasn't struggling through those cold London nights. 'Very good,' Bon replied, his eyes flickering with evil delight. Though Angus added: 'Mine were good. His weren't. I wouldn't touch 'em with a bloody pole!'

In September 1976, AC/DC released their third Australian album, *Dirty Deeds Done Dirt Cheap*, which contained some classic Bon lyrics in songs such as 'Big Balls', 'Ain't No Fun (Waiting 'Round To Be A Millionaire)', 'Ride On', 'Jailbreak' and, of course, the title track, which opened the album. Al Webb raved in *Juke*: '*Dirty Deeds* is still blatant all right, dirt cheap if you like, but done with great musical intelligence and that's what separates the big boys from the little boys.'

Bon knew a thing or two about dirty deeds. At the King of Pop Awards in Melbourne in 1976, he shocked a TV executive when he pulled out a rather large vibrator at the post-show buffet. And Bon chuckled when he recounted how the cops found his 'brag book' after a consensual encounter involving a woman, a Coke bottle and a Polaroid camera. The police found the woman hitchhiking the following day and returned her to Bon's motel room—where they discovered his little black book.

AC/DC returned to Australia at the end of 1976 for what should have been a triumphant homecoming tour. The working title for the tour was 'The Little Cunts Have Done It', but it ended up being named 'A Giant Dose of Rock'n'roll'.

The tour kicked off with a show at Melbourne's Myer Music Bowl, with Bon addressing the crowd: 'Eh,' he smirked, 'what about a few dirty deeds, eh?' And it climaxed with Bon helping Angus bare his bum. The *Juke* reviewer had a great description of Bon's approach: 'Bon Scott himself seemed less stable, running about the stage as if in an effort to dispossess himself of the limitation of only being in the one place at the one time.'

Before the Bowl show, AC/DC did a secret warm-up gig at Richmond's Tiger Lounge, the band room at the Royal Oak Hotel on the corner of Bridge Road and Burnley Street. The place was packed and I was up the front with Irene. I think Bon loved the fact that we had become such great friends. The band blazed through some classic covers, including 'Jailhouse

Rock', 'Roll Over Beethoven' and 'Whole Lotta Shakin' Goin' On'. They were in great form.

Unfortunately, Angus's bare butt got far too much attention. He was just a cheeky schoolboy—'My arse is better looking than my face,' he explained—but country cops treated him like a common criminal, threatening him with arrest if he didn't keep his clothes on. And Sydney's top-rating music station, 2SM—which was owned by the Catholic Church—stopped playing AC/DC's records, with the general manager, Garvin Rutherford, telling the press: 'Members of Australian punk rock group AC/DC must decide if they are strippers or musicians. Until they do, the station will not associate with them in any way.'

And then the band's tour program made its way to talkback radio. On page 8, one of Bon's quotes was wrongly attributed to bass player Mark Evans. The quote was classic Bon: 'I'd like to make enough money so I could fuck Britt Ekland.' It was a little crass, but I don't think that Rod Stewart or his girlfriend would have cared, though the seventies shock jocks were outraged.

In some conservative country areas, AC/DC were literally run out of town. The band's Tamworth show was cancelled two days before the guys were scheduled to play at the town hall, with Tamworth mayor Norman McKellar saying he didn't want the town's youngsters subjected to AC/DC's 'vulgarities'.

Of course, Alderman McKellar had never seen AC/DC live. But he declared, 'I have read things about their concerts which have made my hair stand on end.'

The irony was that the band had played for 800 kids in Tamworth the previous December without incident.

After the Tamworth debacle, another AC/DC gig was cancelled, in Warrnambool in country Victoria. Unfortunately, the 'Giant Dose of Rock'n'roll' turned into a giant dose of drama. No wonder the boys sounded happy to be back in London in 1977.

'Australia is socially and musically a very middle-of-the-road place,' Malcolm told the UK press in March 1977. 'The biggest thing over there is ABBA. We knew when we started out that eventually we would have to get out 'cause we're way too loud for 'em.'

Bon added, 'I think it's very hypocritical banning our records because they are supposedly lewd. Personally, I think they are funnier than they are filthy. I mean, remember all those World War II songs when they marched into battle? Or all those songs by the rugby clubs . . . they're the same, aren't they?'

Bon made a good point.

'We're not corrupting youth, we are merely talking in their language. They don't say, "Play louder," they say, "Fucking play it louder!" We're as subtle as each other.'

Sadly, Mark Evans exited the band in England mid-1977, replaced by Englishman Cliff Williams. Mark was quoted in the press at the time as saying that the decision was mutual and due to 'musical differences', but I knew that Mark wouldn't have voluntarily left. Unfortunately, Bon didn't show Mark due respect when he did interviews with the press a couple of months after his departure. 'The band has improved incredibly,' Bon claimed. 'Whereas before we had only Malcolm's back-up vocals, we now have two back-up vocalists. Cliff's also a better bass player.'

I was sad to see Mark go—he's a lovely guy.

Mark's exit didn't slow AC/DC's international assault. They were hell-bent on conquering hearts and minds and other parts of the anatomy, though Angus lamented to *Sounds* that English girls weren't as easy as their American counterparts. 'Chicks in America come backstage and want to screw you,' Angus explained. 'Chicks here [in the UK] come backstage with their boyfriends and they just want autographs.'

'Whether you screw 'em or not,' Bon added, 'depends on how big their boyfriends are.'

Countdown was a big part of the AC/DC story in Australia. Molly flew to the UK to organise the London leg of the show's 100th episode, which went to air on 3 April 1977. The taping was noteworthy for an unusual boxing match. 'I'm not exactly sure what happened,' Molly admits. 'Leo says it wasn't a punch, but he did push Bon over. I've been in a few punch-ups over the years, but this was definitely one of the stranger bouts—Leo Sayer versus Bon Scott.'

Bon mentioned *Countdown*'s 100th episode when he next caught up with Molly in London, in November 1977, saying, 'It was a really good day because the bar was open the whole time.'

Molly asked Bon if AC/DC changed their act for different markets. 'We're exactly the same,' Bon replied emphatically. 'We are what we are and we ain't gonna change for nobody.'

AC/DC initially focused on the UK and Europe, but then they made some serious inroads in the US in 1977, on the 'Let There Be Rock' tour, and in 1978, promoting their *Powerage* album. 'America has been waiting for a band like us to come along,' Bon declared. Influential American magazine *Cashbox* described *Powerage* as 'the ideal soundtrack for a fist fight'.

Gene Simmons from Kiss saw AC/DC play at the Whisky a Go Go in Los Angeles in August 1977, and Bon says Gene approached the band after the gig and said: 'I dig your band. We're touring in December and I'd like you to tour with us.' AC/DC ended up doing several shows with Kiss on their 'Alive II' tour.

AC/DC's American invasion coincided with Little River Band conquering the US charts. LRB featured Beeb Birtles, who started out in The Valentines' old rivals, Zoot. Bon and Beeb, however, were no longer competing for the same fans. AC/DC's loud, lewd rock was a million miles from LRB's soft rock. As *Cashbox* said, 'If Australian music was a coin, LRB would be heads and AC/DC would be tails.'

Bon didn't dig the West Coast sound that was dominating American radio. He called it 'sickening' and likened it to Australia's love affair with ABBA. 'There was one station that we had there, their logo was "The rock music without the noise" and then they put on Linda Ronstadt, James Taylor and Heart.'

AC/DC were committed to winning over everyone in America—even if they had to do it one fan at a time via their killer live show. When Bon caught up with Molly in November 1977, *Let There Be Rock* had just become the band's first charting album in the US. 'It's number 150 with an arrow,' Bon joked. 'Not quite as fast as a bullet.'

After a tour with Aerosmith, one American reviewer bagged the headliners and praised the support act. 'For a million dollar band, it [Aerosmith] was simply appalling. The opening act from AC/DC was a surprise, or perhaps, a rude awakening . . . a true high-energy band, rock showmanship at its most outrageous. There is nothing serious or important about AC/DC, of course, but the thing is the five of them act like they know that.'

It was a great period for Australian music internationally, and in November 1978 Channel Seven ran a two-hour special called *Taking Australian Music To The World*. The co-producer and talent coordinator was none other than Bon's co-lead singer from The Valentines, Vince Lovegrove. He interviewed LRB, the Bee Gees, Andy Gibb, Helen Reddy and Samantha Sang, and he caught up with Bon and the boys in the US. 'AC/DC are monster drawcards,' Vince told the Australian viewers. 'They're blowing all the bigger names offstage. They just need a hit single and they'll blow the scene there right open.'

To promote their 1979 album, *Highway To Hell*, AC/DC did a show with The Who at Wembley. The show left one English reviewer perplexed. 'A heavy metal archetype overblown to the point where stereotype meets parody . . . is Bon Scott serious or what? Is he just playing out a real-life comic strip of a heavy metal lead singer? Do they smirk when they write those giant three-chord riffs? Or do they just know that the world will love something this crass?'

When AC/DC released the *Highway To Hell* album, Bon and Angus did an interview in the UK, which was reprinted in *Juke*. It showed just how close Bon and Angus had become and what a great double-act they were when it came to dealing with the media.

Question: 'How did you get to be the lovable, well-balanced person you are now?'

Bon: 'I met Angus.'

Angus: 'I have been a reforming influence. You should have seen the man when I first met him. He couldn't speak English—it was all "fuck, cunt, piss, shit". I introduced him to a new side of life. Sent him home with a dictionary.'

Bon: 'He taught me how to say, "Please fuck" and "thank you".'

That article came with a strange coda, which proved eerily prophetic. 'Oddly enough, there does seem to be some truth in Angus, or perhaps the whole band, having taken Bon in hand in an almost fatherly fashion, although he's much the oldest of them at thirty-three,' the writer concluded.

'For all the scraps and scrapes AC/DC are so frequently caught up in, Bon remains the one they feel they have to keep an eye on.'

Legendary American record producer Rick Rubin first heard AC/DC when they played 'Problem Child' on the TV show The Midnight Special *in 1979. Rick was just sixteen and didn't know much about rock'n'roll. 'I only knew that they sounded better than any other band.' Later that year, Rick saw AC/DC live for the first time, when they supported Ted Nugent at Madison Square Garden. He recalls that 'the crowd yanked all the chairs off the floor and piled them into a pyramid in front of the stage. It was a tribute to how great they were'.*

Rick wrote about AC/DC in Rolling Stone's *'Immortals' issue in 2005. 'I'll go on record as saying they're the greatest rock'n'roll band of all time. They didn't write emotional lyrics. They didn't play emotional songs. The emotion is all in that groove. And that groove is timeless.'*

Rick—who produced AC/DC's 1995 album, Ballbreaker— *called* Highway To Hell *'probably the most natural-sounding rock record I've ever heard. There's so little adornment . . . for me, it's the embodiment of rock'n'roll'.*

The last goodbye

Mary

At the start of 1980, I got a call from Bon's ex-wife, Irene. She had news: 'Bon's in town.'

Irene was living in Melbourne with her partner, Nick. In fact, she was pregnant with her first child. And I was living with my boyfriend, Peter.

'Come over,' she said.

Peter and I went to Irene's place the next day. Now, Peter was jealous of everyone, but he got along with Bon. When Bon greeted me at Irene's, he gave me a big hug and a quick grope, but Peter didn't seem to mind. Bon was such a likeable guy; he made everyone feel comfortable.

Bon was wearing an orange Hawaiian shirt. He was definitely in holiday mode, which was, of course, his usual mode.

'Do you think I could come and stay at your place?' Bon whispered to me. Though he remained on great terms with Irene, I don't think he felt comfortable staying with his ex-wife when she was about to become a mum. So, Bon came home with Peter and me, to my shop in Greville Street, Prahran, where we were also living.

I opened the shop in 1978, selling knitwear and lots of men's shirts and pants. Greville Street was a very cool location, with vintage clothing outlets, and my shop was a popular hangout for musicians and members of the cast of the TV show *Prisoner*.

My stepdaughter, Erica, was staying at a friend's place for the summer holidays, so Bon slept in her little room, in a single bunk bed surrounded by blue clouds and fairies.

Bon was in great spirits. He was raving about a book he'd read—John Irving's *The World According To Garp*—and I could tell he was happy to be back in Melbourne.

I called my friend Karin—the girl to whom I had given Bon for her twenty-first birthday—and she came around to catch up. The shop was close to the Station Hotel, so we spent a lot of time there, drinking and chatting. On one of the days at the Station, someone started a fight and Bon jumped in and stopped it. As Judy King's dad would know, Bon was a lover, not a fighter, though he could certainly handle himself. On another occasion, I remember a guy at the pub said something rude to Karin and me. Bon basically kicked him off his chair, and the guy was thrown out. Bon wouldn't start a fight, but he could finish one. He wasn't a tall man but, like Malcolm, he wasn't afraid of anything. Maybe it's a Scottish thing.

During another of Bon's visits to Melbourne in the AC/DC days, we caught up at a gig at Martini's in Carlton. After the show, Bon, Irene, AC/DC's roadie Pat Pickett and I piled into a little car belonging to one of Pat's mates. 'I'm bloody squashed!' Irene complained. The driver, Pat's mate, turned around and slapped Irene, telling her to 'Shut the fuck up!'

We were all stunned, and Bon flew into a blind rage. 'Are you fucking crazy? That's my fucking wife!' Bon and Irene were no longer together, but his old instincts kicked in. A series of blows rained down on the bloke as Bon yelled, 'You hit my fucking missus!' It was very unpleasant.

Like Darcy, Pat Pickett was a legendary roadie. He invented 'the dance of the flaming arseholes', which was popular during AC/DC's early days. Pat would shove toilet paper up his bum and then set it alight. Appropriately, when Angus first saw Pat, he reminded him of the Redhead matches girl.

Like Bon, Pat had a bawdy sense of humour. He once did an interview with a friend's daughter for her school project. One of the questions was, 'Your best friend?' Pat answered, 'My right hand.' Pat also wouldn't take any shit from young bands. He'd say, 'What the fuck are you standing there for, load your fucking gear in!' Or if they were too loud, he'd bark, 'The fucking back wall is just over there, turn your fucking amp down, rock star.' And he also loved rhyming slang. He'd get up and have a 'Berocca and a dapper dan' and put on his fluorescent 'almond rocks'.

Bon had many memorable nights with Pat, none more so than when Bon came home to Pat's place after a gig to find Pat's naked girlfriend gaffer-taped to a table and chair, and Pat unconscious on the floor. 'Thank God you came home!' she yelled at Bon.

After getting set for some passionate lovemaking, Pat had had a joint—and fallen asleep. 'And I can't wake him up!' Bon thought it was hysterical. He had saved another damsel in distress.

At the Station Hotel during Bon's visit at the start of 1980, Bon was drinking Rusty Nails and beers, so all the boys were drinking Rusty Nails and beers. Mark Barnes, who ran the venue, was rapt to see Bon back in town. He made him a weird concoction, some sort of swamp water. It must have been pretty horrid because Bon spat it into the gutter surrounding the bar. It was a strange green colour; I never did find out what was in it.

Mark Barnes was a great publican. He was a musician himself, so he always made sure the bands were paid and looked after with plenty of drinks. Mark had been the bass player in Cam-Pact, alongside Keith Glass, Chris Stockley and Trevor Courtney. All of the guys knew Bon from his early days in Melbourne. On one Valentine's Day at the end of the sixties, The Valentines did an in store appearance at Allans in Collins Street. Cam-Pact heard about it, hired a 1928 Chevy and waited for the band to come out of the store. When Bon and the boys walked out—in their orange chiffon suits—the Cam-Pact crew pounced, shooting them with water pistols filled with blue dye. It was Cam-Pact's version of the Valentine's Day Massacre.

When The Valentines' manager, Bill Joseph, heard about the incident he was furious that the Cam-Pact guys hadn't let him in on the prank—if they had, Bill would have got the press down there to cover the ambush.

Another night when Bon was in town in 1980, we decided to go to Bombay Rock in Brunswick, which was the big gig at the time. I can't recall who was playing; it might have been Mi-Sex. Because we'd been drinking at the Station, we decided to catch a taxi, but one of Bon's friends had a ute, so Bon travelled from Prahran to Brunswick in the back of a ute.

We met out the front, and I could tell that something wasn't quite right. The bouncer wouldn't let Bon in.

'What do you mean?' I asked.

'He can't come in,' the bouncer said. 'He's got tattoos.'

The bouncer had no idea who Bon was, and Bon was never the sort of guy to play the *Don't you know who I am?* card.

Fortunately, the legendary booking agent Frank Stivala, who ran the venue with Michael Gudinski, appeared. 'What are you doing?' he reprimanded the bouncer. 'It's fucking Bon Scott, let him in!'

That was one of the only times I saw Bon unwilling to accept an apology. 'Nuh, mate,' he said. 'You weren't going to let me in before; I'm not going to accept your apologies now, just because I'm "somebody".'

He was so angry, he refused to go into the club's VIP section, which in reality was just the upstairs section of the venue, with tables and chairs. 'What do you mean?' I pleaded with Bon. 'We can sit down!'

'Nuh, I'm not going up there.'

After the night at Bombay Rock, I called my friend Margaret in Adelaide. 'Get yourself over here and get yourself a good root—Bon's in town!' It wasn't a very ladylike thing to say, but Margaret got the message. Bon spent a couple of nights with Margaret, before heading home to Perth.

Many years later, to mark what would have been Bon's sixtieth birthday, Vince Lovegrove interviewed some people who had known Bon. Ross Wilson talked about an encounter he'd had when Bon was coming to see me at my shop in Greville Street, Prahran.

'He meandered across the street towards me through the hot, dry, Melbourne summer day,' Ross recalled. '"Hi, man," I said, but he just smiled softly and blankly at me and continued on his way. Something seemed to be on his mind. When I thought about it later, I reckon it's probable that Bon was back in town checking out earlier haunts where it all began for him, touching base with friends and places of earlier years, before he left this plane.

'"See ya, man," I said. Except, I didn't. Two months later, I read about his death in London. I was surprised, though no less sad about it.'

It's rather poetic to think that Bon was on some sort of tragic farewell tour, going to all the Australian cities he'd called home—Perth, Melbourne, Sydney and Adelaide—saying goodbye to loved ones because he knew he was going to check out soon after.

It's also ridiculous. And things aren't always what they seem. I vividly remember what Bon had to say after he bumped into Ross Wilson. He came into my shop and said: 'You won't believe who I just saw—that arsehole Ross Wilson! He never used to talk to me before, and now he wants to be my mate. So, I ignored him.'

I spent a week with Bon, and I can tell you that he was in great spirits. He was happy and healthy. He enjoyed plenty of drinks, but he wasn't out of control. Later, there were rumours about Bon having liver cancer. Maybe the doctors had suggested that he needed to take care of his liver, I don't know, but to me, Bon looked normal.

Bon was also really positive about AC/DC's future. He was particularly excited about the band's next album; he knew it was going to be a smash.

'I know the Americans are going to love it,' he told me.

That album was *Back In Black*.

Bon had done an interview with *RAM* in 1979. 'What do you think I do it for?' he said. 'The money or the music? I just do it for the glamour. The women and the whiskey . . . what else is there in life?'

There was nothing to be sad about. In Bon's eyes, everything was great. He'd always dreamed of making it big in America, and he was now on the verge of doing just that. And once he'd cracked America, he could do whatever he wanted: settle down, have a home base, maybe start a family. We chatted about these things when Bon was in Melbourne. He was excited about the future.

That homecoming trip was Bon's way of saying, 'Mate, I'm going to be busy for the next year or two, so let's catch up now. The next time you see me, I'll be really, really famous.' Indeed, in Perth, Bon told his mum that he was going to be a millionaire.

'It's going to happen,' Bon had said to be me, smiling. 'It's really going to happen.'

Mary's Bon and Mary's Pete.

Mary: 'Pete's T-shirt actually belonged to Bon.'

Mary: 'This is one of my favourite photos of Bon, coming out of the bathroom.
I still have this framed on my wall.'

Partying at Mary's shop. Mary, Peter, Bon and Karin.

Still partying at the shop. Margaret, Bon and Karin.

AC/DC's hard work in the UK was paying off. When the Highway To Hell album was released in 1979, the headline in New Musical Express (NME) blazed 'The Greatest Album Ever Made' (in smaller type was the disclaimer 'In Australia'). The glowing review stated that AC/DC 'are a band who practise the science of overstatement to a ludicrous degree and succeed'.

Write on

Mary

I can't imagine that many modern rock stars sit in their hotel rooms after a show penning a letter to their mum or their friends. But Bon was a wonderful letter writer.

'Hello Spunk', his letters would often start.

Angus spoke about Bon's love of communicating in an interview with UK magazine *Sounds* in 1980. 'He made a lot of friends everywhere and was always in contact with them. Weeks before Christmas, he would have piles of cards and he always wrote to anyone that he knew, keeping them informed.'

I would eagerly await Bon's correspondence and it would always amuse and entertain me, as well as provide an insight into the not-so-glamorous world of showbiz.

Bon was a fan of rhyming slang. Poms were 'to-and-froms'; Sydney was 'Steak & Kidney'. And his sense of humour was always wicked. Even at Christmas he was cheeky, sending me a song called 'Jingle Balls'. And when AC/DC were recording their second album, *T.N.T.*, Bon spoke about a new song called 'She's Got The Jack', 'which may get us castrated by women's lib'.

Angus's girlfriend, Heather, later filled me in on the inspiration for the song, which became known by its shorter title, 'The Jack'.

The band was having a barbecue at their Lansdowne Road house in 1975 and, of course, there were plenty of ladies roaming around. At one point, Heather looked up to see Bon and one of the women having sex in the backyard. Nothing unusual about that.

Later, Malcolm and his girlfriend had a tiff inside the house, and she stormed outside to find a rather drunken Bon in the backyard. Bon was now alone and, being a gentleman, he comforted Malcolm's girlfriend. Perhaps he took the comforting a little too far. One thing led to another and—unknown to Malcolm—Bon and Malcolm's girlfriend also ended up having sex in the backyard.

Later that night, Malcolm and his girl reconciled.

The following week, Heather accompanied AC/DC on a tour to Adelaide, riding in the band's old bus, which always broke down. Before they left, Malcolm's girlfriend handed Heather a note.

'When you get a chance, please pass this on to Mal,' she requested.

In Adelaide, the boys were staying with Cold Chisel. Once they got settled, they started setting up to have a jam, and Heather thought this was a good time to give Malcolm the note. It contained the confession that his girlfriend had slept with Bon. Not only that; she had VD and she was worried she might have passed it on to Malcolm. This revelation did not surprise either Malcolm or Bon. They were both 'pissing razor blades', as the saying goes, and aware that they had caught something rather nasty.

And how did Malcolm react? He laughed. He handed the note to Bon, and he laughed, too. Bon then started a slow bluesy jam; the boys joined in, and Bon started singing the twisted tale of an unforgettable barbecue. And 'The Jack' was officially born.

In 1975, I moved to England—and Bon missed my farewell. When I got to London, there was a letter waiting for me, which Bon said he'd written 'whilst on my kneez'.

He'd got the day of my departure wrong. '. . . I thought you were leaving on Monday,' he wrote. 'Felt such a cunt . . .' He also said he'd been in everybody's bad books lately.

AC/DC always wanted to be an international band. Bon was buzzing when John Peel, the legendary English DJ, revealed he was a fan.

'[He] recons [*sic*] we're the band England needs,' Bon said in a letter to me. He didn't know how much longer they'd be in Australia but hoped it wouldn't be long. I gathered there were some unpaid taxes.

Australia was never big enough for AC/DC. 'Still no word on Europe but it shouldn't be too long,' Bon declared in another note. He reckoned the band was 'copping the same shit week in and out' in Melbourne.

Bon and AC/DC were ambitious, but he never got a big head. He was always beautifully self-deprecating. He doubted if he'd be still in Melbourne when I got back from London.

'. . . us stars are always jetting round the country earning thousands of cents,' he informed me.

AC/DC did a big gig at Melbourne's Festival Hall on Anzac Day 1975, with Skyhooks, Split Enz and Bob Hudson. Tickets cost $2.70. Split Enz were booed—Australians were struggling to understand the band's quirky pop—but AC/DC were a smash hit.

'The band was an incredible success,' Lawrie Masterson wrote in *The Herald*. 'Scott was dragged from the stage four times and fans showed their appreciation by ripping his overalls to shreds.'

'It was the wildest concert we've ever played at,' Bon told the paper.

Bon lost his white overalls and bared his bum to the crowd. He had to run off stage for a costume change—reappearing in a Tarzan outfit. 'His next trick was to swing across the stage on a rope,' Lawrie reported. 'But his aim was out and again he landed in the crowd.'

Bon loved everything about that show—apart from the fact that AC/DC weren't the headlining act. He longed for the band to do their own Festival Hall show. 'The trouble is getting a good support band,' he explained in a letter to me. He reckoned the best support band in the country was AC/DC, 'or I should say *was* us'. The band supported Skyhooks at a Festival Hall concert and scored full marks from a couple of newspapers. Not so the headlining act.

Bon was certainly not a Hooks fan. I think he was jealous of their success. (Their debut album, *Living In The 70's*, spent sixteen weeks at number one and became the biggest-selling local album ever to that point.) And I don't think that the

Hooks treated their support bands very well. 'They're a pain in the arse,' Bon wrote, adding that they weren't good enough to support AC/DC. He even jokingly proposed beating them up on stage for an encore.

Ironically, AC/DC is Greg Macainsh's all-time favourite Australian band. When the *Herald Sun* asked musicians to rank their favourite local bands in 2015, the Skyhooks bass player and songwriter placed AC/DC at number one. 'Even back in 1974 at the Chelsea Civic Centre, it was obvious that the Youngs possessed a single-mindedness that was going to take them a long way to the shop if you wanted that sausage roll,' Greg said. 'I continued to buy each new release as a tithe to the church that Malcolm and Angus built. The last two Bons [*Powerage* and *Highway To Hell*] and the first two Brians [*Back In Black* and *For Those About To Rock We Salute You*] are the vinyls to have.'

AC/DC came in at number one in the *Herald Sun* poll. Music writer Cameron Adams, who compiled the results, wrote that they 'romped home. AC/DC score more votes than anyone, demonstrating the cross-generational appeal and respect that's seen them become Australia's most successful musical export'. John Farnham said: 'AC/DC are the best rock'n'roll band that ever existed. Bon Scott was incredible. "It's A Long Way To The Top" is probably the best rock song ever written.'

Bon knew that it was a long way to the top, and he wanted to conquer the world before he settled down. In a letter to me in London, he mentioned that he'd bumped into an old girlfriend named Sandie at the Hard Rock in Melbourne. Bon was pleased to see her, but thought she wanted a husband: '. . . I ain't goin back (too young I am)'.

Later, Bon described the chicks in England as 'outta sight'. And he meant literally, lamenting that his love life was suffering on the road. 'It's kinda painful,' he added, though, 'love will prevail.'

In a postcard to Darce and Gab, Bon spoke of the band's two-week stint in Sweden. He had a great time but declared the Swedes' reputation for 'being promiscuous' was 'a load of shit': 'I had to pull myself twice!'

Life on the road could be lonely. In one letter he thanked me for remembering his birthday: 'Not many did.'

Bon enjoyed receiving fan mail, even if it was not always positive. He got a kick out of one letter from a woman who believed Bon was a bad influence on Angus. Maybe she was fooled by the school uniform and thought that Angus was actually still at school? 'Bon Scott, I hate you,' the letter started. 'You're a dirty old man and you're leading poor little Angus astray. What is he going to become after being in a band with you?'

Bon was disappointed that the letter did not include a return address. 'Otherwise, I might have gone around and screwed her.'

Fans today understand that AC/DC are one of the biggest bands of all time and Bon is a rock idol, so they probably assume that Bon was rolling in cash, but during AC/DC's early years they actually did it tough. The title of one of AC/DC's songs said it all: 'Ain't No Fun (Waiting 'Round To Be A Millionaire)'.

When I was living in London, Bon asked me to buy some shoes for him, a pair of blue suede bodgie shoes, and send them home to him. But then he told me not to bother—'I just can't get the money together.'

But Bon loved life on the road. He told an American interviewer in 1978: 'It keeps you fit—the alcohol, nasty women, sweat on stage, bad food. It's all very good for you.' In his card to Darce and Gab, he apologised for not writing sooner, explaining, 'I've been stoned for about three months solid.' He said there was enough hash in London to keep Melbourne 'stoned for ten fuckin years'.

He sent me one letter from the Bond Court Hotel in Cleveland, Ohio, on the 1977 'Let There Be Rock' tour, telling me how much he was looking forward to the band relocating to the US from mid-1978: '. . . I can't wait. I wanna kick ass, baby.'

He was like a wide-eyed, naïve tourist about his travels in the US. In a letter to me in August 1977, he described 'the size, speed and Americanism' of Texas: 'exactly how it is in all the TV and movie shows . . . the place is full of freaks.'

Bon would always mention what the band was up to, but never in a big-noting, 'look at me' way. He was genuinely proud when the band started making inroads in Europe, where he said people were 'starved for rock'n'roll'. After ten days in Sweden he wrote that 'people loved the band'. He was also itching to tell me that AC/DC sold out five Monday nights at The Marquee in London.

I know that Bon kept all of my cards and letters. I would have loved to have seen them because they documented my life for a few years. But most of Bon's personal possessions mysteriously disappeared after his death.

I often cry when I read Bon's letters and cards. One particular Christmas card gets me every time. 'To my friend Mary,' Bon wrote. 'Hope we're friends forever.' He wished me a Merry Christmas and 'a Happy 1980'.

The American edition of Rolling Stone *magazine called 'Highway To Hell' one of the 500 Greatest Songs of All Time. '"Highway" is the last will and testament of Scott: When he yells, "Don't stop me," right before Angus Young's guitar solo, it's clear that no one could.'*

One of a kind

Mary

At the beginning of 1980, the week after Bon was in Melbourne, I received a package in the mail. It was from Bon and contained some *Highway To Hell* T-shirts, stickers, a singlet and a windcheater. On the back of the windcheater is a list of the final shows of AC/DC's European tour in 1979:

17 Dec—Hammersmith Odeon
18 Dec—Southampton Gaumont
19 Dec—Brighton Centre
20/21 Dec—Birmingham Odeon

Bon's note with the package included the question, 'How's the kidneys, Peter?', which was a cheeky reference to all the drinking he'd done with my boyfriend when they'd been together in Melbourne.

Bon was no longer in town, but it felt like he was still here. I chuckled when I picked up the 19 January 1980 copy of *Juke*, which featured a retrospective piece on bubblegum pop. 'If you think disco's dumb,' the paper stated, 'you shoulda been around in the bubblegum era when bands looked like this.'

Accompanying the article was a photo of The Valentines.

It was a busy start to a new year and a new decade. Angus had just married his Dutch girlfriend, Ellen. In Australia, it was summer, my shop was busy, and Irene was pregnant and about to go into labour. We were chatting on the phone about Bon. It was strange—it was like he was still with us. I hung up and started writing a letter to Bon to thank him for the package. Then the phone rang. It was Irene again.

'Bon is dead,' she said.

'What?'

'Bon is dead.'

The rest of the conversation is a blur. Irene didn't have any more details. Malcolm had called Bon's mum, Isa, and Isa got her daughter-in-law, Val, to call Irene. Malcolm later said the call to Mrs Scott was 'the most difficult thing I've ever had to do'. Bon's network of friends relayed the news. Irene called Betty King; Betty called Gabby and Darce.

No one could believe it.

This can't be right, I thought. *I just saw Bon three weeks ago. He can't be dead.*

Angus was also stunned, later telling a radio interviewer: 'It was disbelief at first. I heard from a girlfriend of his. She was in panic. Then another girlfriend of his called . . . I got hold of the guy who was managing us at the time [Peter Mensch]. He thought it was just a rumour.'

Angus rang the hospital, but the staff wouldn't give him any information. Then Peter Mensch called back. It was true. 'It was like losing a member of your family,' Angus said simply. 'That's the only way to describe it.'

Angus, a teetotaller, knew that Bon loved to party. 'He used to worry me at times, but Malcolm would say, "Bon's one of those people, he has a great night out, then he has eight hours' sleep and while everyone else has their heads in buckets, Bon's bouncing around looking for the next party."

'Even though he did like to drink and have a bit of a crazy time, he was always there when you needed him.'

I ran across the road to the shop belonging to the music writer known as Doctor Pepper, David Pepperell, to tell him I was closing my shop for the day. I tried to call Bon's mum. Fifa Riccobono from Alberts, AC/DC's Australian label, was dealing with all the phone calls to the family, but Isa said, 'No, no, I know Mary,' and eventually I got to speak with her.

I really felt for Fifa. She was trying to look after the band and Bon's family while fielding media inquiries from all over the world. She did a great job, which was not easy because she also loved Bon and was devastated by his death.

The whole thing was traumatic. My partner Peter's ex-wife— the mother of my stepdaughter—had died a month earlier from an asthma attack. Now, Bon was dead. I didn't know what to think or what to do.

The letter I'd written to Bon was sitting on my desk in the shop, ready to post.

Sydney's *Daily Telegraph* said: 'When Bon Scott died in London yesterday, a little piece of Australian rock history ended.'

RAM ran a special tribute to Bon: 'Bon Scott: Tribute To A Fallen Warrior'. Harry Vanda and George Young—who produced every AC/DC album that Bon made, apart from *Highway To Hell*—took out a full-page ad, which stated:

A Great Singer,
A Great Lyricist,
A Great Friend,
One Of A Kind
We'll miss you.
—Harry & George

Vince Lovegrove wrote about his 'last heart-to-heart with Bon', after an AC/DC gig in Atlanta, Georgia, during the 'Powerage' tour on 11 August 1978. Vince called it 'one of those truth sessions that friends have after a drinking spree, and Bon and I had a few in our fifteen-year friendship'.

I still get emotional when I think about that article. And a little bit angry. Vince portrayed Bon as an unhappy person, which was simply not true.

In the article, Vince was buzzing after the show, saying 'the original wild colonial boys' had blown Cheap Trick off the Symphony Hall stage, and 'Bon was struttin' across the floorboards like the eternal Peter Pan'. (Coincidentally, Bon came from the same town in Scotland, Kirriemuir, as *Peter Pan* author J.M. Barrie.)

After the gig, Vince and Bon returned to the Peachtree Plaza Hotel, 'a fucking long way from North Fremantle where we first met'.

'I'm getting tired of it all,' Vince claimed Bon confided in him.

'We were both wasted,' Vince wrote in his *RAM* piece. 'Totally, there were no inhibitions.'

Vince said he was shocked by Bon's confession. But he quoted Bon: 'No way, Vinnie, I really am getting tired. I love it, you know that. It's only rock'n'roll and I like it. But I want to have a base. It's just the constant pressures of touring that's fucking it. I've been on the road for thirteen years. Rock'n'roll, you know that's all there is. But I can't hack the rest of the shit that goes with it.'

Vince said he'd never seen Bon like this.

I was angry about the article because I believe this was possibly the only time Bon had ever been vulnerable with Vince, and he then used that against Bon. Sure, they'd been in a band together for four years, but I doubt that Bon and Vince had many 'truth sessions'; that wasn't the nature of their relationship.

Years later, Vince was working with an American film producer, trying to make a movie about Bon's life. She emailed me, saying, 'Bon was in a really dark place; he was going to leave the band.' Vince had told her that, and it was total crap.

Ozzy Osbourne wrote a song called 'Suicide Solution', which he said was an anti-alcohol eulogy for Bon. But this wasn't a suicide; it was just a tragic accident. The official cause listed on Bon's death certificate was 'acute alcohol poisoning'. The inquest was conducted three days after Bon's death, with the assistant deputy coroner ruling 'death by misadventure'.

Bon did not have a death wish. Indeed, just two months before he died, he did an interview in Glasgow. 'I've been on the road for fifteen years,' he said. 'And I have no intent to stop. We meet a lot of people, we drink lots of stuff and have lots of fun.'

And around the time that Vince caught up with Bon and AC/DC in the US, *Juke* journalist Simon Balderstone asked Angus how Bon was going. 'Bon is fine,' Angus replied. 'We call him the old man, but he's always there. And he will be in the future.'

When Bon spoke to Vince, he would have been exhausted after AC/DC's show—the 55th show of the 'Powerage' tour. Vince made it look like his meeting with Bon was all doom and gloom and Bon was depressed, but Bon was obviously in a reflective, playful mood. To surprise Vince, Bon called The Valentines' old drummer, Doug Lavery, who was living in America with his wife, Pauline, and drumming with Rick Nelson's Stone Canyon Band. Bon and Vince left a rude message on Doug's answering machine, and then called Pauline's sister, Valerie.

Of course, life on the road is not easy. Every rock star gets tired and lonely and wants to be at home with family and friends—but that doesn't mean they're depressed. In December 1978, Bon did an interview with Melbourne *Sun* rock writer Pat Bowring. The article started: 'If Bon Scott is lucky, he'll see his parents in Perth at Christmas. "I haven't seen them for three years. I hope they recognise me," he said.' Bon missed the important people in his life, but he loved fronting AC/DC. And three weeks before he died, he was itching to get into the studio and make the band's next album. He knew it was going to be great and the band would take America by storm.

At least Vince managed to sum up Bon accurately: 'I'd never known anyone as loyal as Bon when it came to friendships,' he wrote. 'He never forgot anyone.' He recounted the story of

Bon riding his motorbike from Adelaide to Melbourne 'just to say hello to The Valentines' old roadie, Darcy'.

Vince's article wasn't the only newspaper piece that made me angry. 'Rock Star Drank Himself To Death' blazed the headline in one Australian paper. 'Could Have Had 2 Bottles Of Scotch.' The opening sentence referred to Bon as the 'outrageous lead singer' of AC/DC.

I was a mess in the days after Bon's death, and the stuff in the papers just made me more emotional. I think I was so upset, I even rang one newspaper and abused a journalist. So many things just sensationalised Bon's life, making it look like he was a wild rock star who led a debauched existence. Sure, there was some truth in that, but there was much more substance to Bon. When a rock star dies tragically, people just see the legend and not the real person.

I felt for Bon's family. His little brother, Graeme, was in Thailand, and found out about Bon's death via telegram.

Heartbreakingly, Isa later confided to me: 'You didn't tell Bon what to do. I just said I didn't like him drinking. But when they get to that stage, they don't listen, do they?'

Ted Albert, the driving force behind the Alberts empire, wrote to Bon's parents. 'We have lost a really good friend,' he said. 'There are not many people in the entertainment world, unfortunately, who you could call a friend . . . but Bon was one of the real exceptions—a genuine person with a generous nature and a real wish to make others happy. A gentleman in the truest sense.'

As Vince said, 'Just when the band was on the brink of worldwide superstar status, the Bon fire burned out . . . and, fuck it, for all of us, it burnt out too soon.'

A few days after Bon's death, the band found out that *Highway To Hell* had gone platinum in America, having sold one million copies.

Bon was officially a rock'n'roll star.

No one knew what was going to happen to AC/DC without Bon. I just felt so sad for my friend, but I also knew how much work the boys had done, and that it would be devastating if the band finished. A spokesman for AC/DC's record company in the UK said, 'He was very essential to the band's image and sound and he will be almost irreplaceable. But the rest of the guys are just too stunned at this stage to have even considered what their next move will be.'

RAM editor, Anthony O'Grady, wrote a personal piece, calling Bon 'one of the most genuinely gentle and considerate people I've ever met. With Bon, you were either a friend for life or someone who didn't deserve to be spoken to'.

Anthony was rocked by Bon's death. 'To me, I always believed that, somehow, he'd just float to the top, giggling and ready to do it all over again. He always had before.

'Except, this time, he just floated away.'

Backstage in 1991 at AC/DC's 'The Razors Edge' tour.
Mary: 'Malcolm organised all the boys to get together for this photo with my son Paris.'

Mary and Malcolm Young backstage in Perth
during AC/DC's 'Black Ice' tour in 2010.
Mary: 'Malcolm is one of the nicest people I have ever met in my life.'

Hanging out backstage in Perth.

Mary: 'Another pic from the "Black Ice" tour. This is me and my daughter Erica with Angus Young and Bon's younger brother, Graeme.'

In 2005, journalist Richard Jinman asked Bon's biographer Clinton Walker about Alistair Kinnear, the last person to see Bon alive. 'No one spoke to him before or after the event [Bon's death],' Clinton said. 'He just doesn't seem to exist.'

But soon after, UK rock magazine Metal Hammer *tracked down Alistair, who told the magazine that he met Bon through their mutual friend, Silver Smith. On 18 February, the manager of The Only Ones, Zena Kakoulli, invited Alistair to the debut gig for her sister's band, Lonesome No More (featuring Billy Duffy on guitar, who would later form The Cult), at the Music Machine in Camden Town. He invited Silver; she was busy, but suggested that Bon might like to go.*

'It was a great party, and Bon and I both drank far too much,' Alistair says. 'However, I did not see him take any drugs.'

Alistair drove Bon home after the gig, but Bon's London girlfriend [Anna Baba] wasn't home. 'I was unable to wake Bon, so I rang Silver for advice. She said that he passed out quite frequently and that it was best just to leave him to sleep it off.'

Alistair drove to his flat in Overhill Road, East Dulwich. He was unable to move Bon, so he reclined the passenger seat of his little Renault, covered Bon with a blanket and left a note with his address and phone number. 'It must have been four or five a.m. at that time, and I slept until about eleven.' Alistair says he was woken by a friend, Leslie Loads. Still hungover, he asked Leslie to check on Bon. Leslie said that no one was in the car, so Alistair assumed that Bon had caught a taxi home. About 7.30 p.m., Alistair was alarmed to find Bon still in his car, 'obviously in a very bad way, and not breathing'. He drove him to King's College Hospital, where Bon was pronounced dead on arrival.

'It has since been speculated that Bon choked on his own vomit, but I can neither confirm nor deny this . . . there was no vomit in the car.'

Alistair claims that Silver told him the following day that Bon had been receiving treatment for liver damage and had missed several appointments. 'I wish that I had known this at the time.'

Alistair denied he had 'disappeared', saying he had been working as a musician on the Costa del Sol for twenty-two years. 'I truly regret Bon's death,' he said. 'What I'd like to pass on from this unfortunate experience is the idea that we should all take better care of our friends and err on the side of caution when we don't know all the facts.'

Since doing that interview, it seems that Alistair has again disappeared. Word is he vanished while on a fishing trip.

'Whatever you do, don't stop'

Mary

AC/DC hadn't played in Australia for more than two years. Their last local gig was a jam at the Bondi Lifesaver on 8 July 1977. Bon's final gig was his funeral in Fremantle on 1 March 1980.

Unfortunately, Irene couldn't attend. The day before Bon's funeral, she gave birth to her first son, Lee. I can't imagine what Irene was going through. Unbelievable joy and utter devastation. Darce and Gabby also couldn't make it; flights to Perth in those days were ridiculously expensive and they couldn't afford to go. I had to borrow money from my friend Margaret. She knew I had to be there.

I flew to Perth and caught a taxi to Fremantle Cemetery. I sat on a gravestone, alone, before everyone arrived. I had no idea what was going to happen. It was the first funeral I'd been to for someone I truly loved. It certainly wasn't a big rock'n'roll production. If you happened to be walking by, you wouldn't have realised that a rock icon was being farewelled. It was a low-key affair; the AC/DC guys and Harry Vanda and George Young were the only rock stars in the congregation.

A few fans walked quietly behind Bon's coffin. Bon's first serious girlfriend, Maria Short, was there with her husband. It was nice to see Maria, whom I hadn't seen since she dropped in to see Bon at The Valentines' Toorak Road flat at the end of the sixties. Maria—who ended up owning a fashion boutique in Perth—had met Bon at The Spektors' very first gig in Perth in 1965 when she was seventeen. She told me that she thought I was going out with Bon during The Valentines days. 'No,' I smiled, 'that didn't happen until later.' At the funeral, I did meet a woman who had dated Bon for a week or two while he was with The Valentines. She was deeply moved. That was the thing about Bon—he loved a lot of women and they loved him forever.

The priest spoke some hollow words—it was obvious that he didn't know much about Bon or his life—and that was pretty much it. No one else spoke. The service wasn't really a celebration of Bon's life.

No one could believe that Bon was no longer with us. I was struck by the thought that I would never hear his wild cackle again. That wild cackle, wicked smile and those sparkling eyes. There were no warnings and no goodbyes. As *Rolling Stone* bluntly put it: 'One week in 1980, Angus and Malcolm Young were running through ideas with frontman Bon Scott in a London rehearsal studio. The next Tuesday, Scott drank himself to death.'

After the funeral, Malcolm and Angus took me in their car to Bon's parents' place for the wake. Isa and Chick were lovely people, and this was a happy occasion, a get-together of people who loved Bon. It was particularly poignant to see the five chairs that Isa had put out for the AC/DC members. Of course, a key member of the band was missing, but Chick urged the boys to soon fill the seat. 'You've got to find someone else, you know that,' Bon's dad told Malcolm. 'Whatever you do, don't stop.'

'That was good for us,' Angus later said. 'It didn't make it feel like we were cheating on him.'

Molly suggested on *Countdown* that The Easybeats' Stevie Wright would become AC/DC's new lead singer. Many people thought it was insensitive, coming so soon after Bon's passing, but Molly was pragmatic. 'Life goes on. If I dropped dead I'd expect *Countdown* to announce a replacement immediately and keep going.'

At the wake, we had sandwiches and cups of tea with Bon's mum and dad. Unfortunately, Bon's brother Graeme wasn't there. He was not coping well with Bon's death and couldn't face the funeral. Isa was very concerned that he hadn't turned up. 'Don't worry,' I reassured her. 'He'll eventually come home.' And he did, two days later.

Just before he died, Bon wrote a letter to Graeme, revealing that he was writing lyrics for AC/DC's new album. The letter followed Graeme all around the world, to Bangkok, to Melbourne, and eventually to Alberts in Sydney. Graeme finally got the letter in 1984—four years after Bon died.

It's funny the things you remember. At the funeral, Phil Rudd asked me: 'Have you got any rotten bananas?' He then gave me a recipe for banana bread, scribbling it on a scrap of paper. (I made it when I got home and Phil was right, it was delicious.)

After the wake, Phil took me sailing, which was a beautiful way to celebrate Bon's life. It was a hot sunny day and I could feel Bon in the breeze. Phil told me a funny story about a day he spent at Disneyland with Bon. They decided to go to Disneyland because a fan had given them a joint after an AC/DC gig. It turned out the joint was laced with angel dust and both Bon and Phil freaked out. There they were, two 'wild' rockers in the middle of Disneyland, holding hands, waiting until the drug wore off.

After the boat trip with Phil, I had dinner with the band, then I caught the last plane home to Melbourne. It was a surreal day. On the flight home, I thought about my friend Bon. He loved many women I know he loved me. And I know he loved Irene.

On his final visit to Melbourne, he told my friend Margaret that there were three women in his life that he truly loved: his mother, Irene and me. That was the last thing he said to Margaret.

'Wasn't it good that he came back to his old roots?' Margaret remarked after Bon's death.

'Yes, it was.'

Margaret has a wonderful way with words.

In an interview with the US edition of Rolling Stone, Angus said, 'I was sad for Bon. I didn't even think about the band. We'd been with Bon all that time; we'd seen more of him than his family did.'

But the Youngs had a remarkable work ethic, with Malcolm adding: 'I thought, "Well, fuck this, I'm not gonna sit around mopin' all fuckin' year." So I just rang up Angus and said, "Do you wanna come back and rehearse?" This was about two days afterward.'

AC/DC replaced Bon with Brian Johnson—the singer Bon had admired in 1973 when Fraternity (then known as Fang) played with Geordie in the UK.

Brian's first album with AC/DC was Back In Black, which Rolling Stone said had 'the relentless logic of a sledgehammer. Back In Black might be the purest distillation of hard rock ever'.

It was the best-reviewed AC/DC album in the pages of Rolling Stone, with David Fricke saying Bon's 'untimely demise seems to have lit a roaring fire under this Australian band. Back In Black is not only the best of AC/DC's six American albums, it's the apex of heavy-metal art: the first LP since Led Zeppelin II that captures all the blood, sweat and arrogance of the genre. In other words, Back In Black kicks like a mutha'.

'Imagine how we felt'

Mary

I bought a copy of *Back In Black*, the AC/DC album that came out just five months after Bon's death. But I've never been able to listen to it.

It was a smash hit, entering the UK charts at number one, topping the Australian charts and reaching number four in the US. And the first single, 'You Shook Me All Night Long', became the band's first Top 40 hit in the US. When the album was released, three of Bon's AC/DC albums re-entered the UK charts: *Highway To Hell*, *If You Want Blood You've Got It* and *Let There Be Rock*. AC/DC were the first band since The Beatles to have four albums in the British Top 100 in the same week.

And *Back In Black* stayed on the *Billboard* charts for more than two-and-a-half years.

The band had become the success Bon dreamed it would be.

Seven months after Bon died, a concert movie, *AC/DC: Let There Be Rock*, was released. Dave Grohl later told *Q* magazine: 'A big rock'n'roll moment for me as a teenager was going to see AC/DC's *Let There Be Rock* movie. That was the first time

I heard music that made me want to break shit. After the first number in that movie ['Live Wire'] that was maybe the first moment in my life where I really felt like a punk.'

Filmed at a gig in Paris on 9 December 1979, the film also featured an interview with Bon, who was wearing a black leather jacket with a white scarf. He spoke about how he would sing in the shower when he was a kid, and his mum would tell him off. 'Bon, if you can't sing proper songs, shut up. Don't sing this rock'n'roll garbage!'

'And now, of course, she loves it very much.'

The interviewer concluded his chat with Bon by mentioning that 'the other boys of the band say that you're great, but, uh, a little special. Do you know what they mean by that?'

'I'm a special drunkard,' Bon said, smiling. 'I drink too much.'

It's an incredibly poignant line. And I have to say I get very emotional when I see Bon talking about how much he loves the women in his life. 'Women are lovely,' he says. 'God's gift to man.'

Men?

'Men are all right. You shake their hand, say hello. But women are special. You can hug them.'

AC/DC toured Australia with Brian Johnson in 1981 and 1988, but I couldn't bring myself to go. Darce saw 1981's infamous Myer Music Bowl show in Melbourne and his one-sentence review seemed to sum it up: 'The backing track was right on, but everything else was not.'

AC/DC returned for 'The Razors Edge' tour in October 1991. My son, Paris, was just nine, but he'd become an AC/DC fan and wanted to see them. My friend Christine found out where they were staying, and when I called the hotel the receptionist said, 'No, they're not staying here, but you can leave a message if you like.'

And Malcolm called back later that day.

It was great to catch up because I always got on well with Malcolm. He invited me to lunch and we talked about Bon.

'How come you've never come to see us?' Malcolm asked.

'I just couldn't, without Bon . . .'

'Well, imagine how we felt.'

Malcolm organised our tickets. Seeing the band do a stadium show was a big thrill. And Paris was just so excited, so I was excited for him. After the show, we went backstage, where Malcolm introduced me to Brian. 'This is Mary, she was really close to Bon.' Brian was really friendly and open; I couldn't help but like him.

There weren't many people backstage, so it was a very friendly atmosphere. Malcolm handed out T-shirts and hats. Everyone was good to Paris, taking photos with him and his mate. (His mate learned a valuable lesson that night—when you're having your photo taken with a famous band, make sure you don't have your cap over your face.)

We ended up going to two shows. I loved it, and I've seen every Australian tour since. An AC/DC show is a joyous experience for fans; for me, it's both happy and sad. I can't help but enjoy it because the band is just so great, but I cry at every AC/DC show. I just miss him so much.

I was very emotional when I saw an AC/DC show in Paris, at the Stade de France, on the 'Black Ice' tour in 2010. It's a huge stadium and nearly 100,000 people were there. I just couldn't watch the show, because I was overwhelmed by the feeling that Bon should have been there. By the time I saw the Berlin show four days later, I was coping better. Bon would have loved doing such big shows. And people still love his songs.

During the 'Black Ice' tour, I also got to see a show in Perth with Bon's brother, Graeme, which was a special experience. Graeme doesn't outwardly show his emotions, but I know that he thinks about Bon every day.

During that tour, Angus's wife, Ellen, and Malcolm's wife, Linda, and Fifa from Alberts went to visit Bon's mum, Isa. She was mentally alert, but she didn't want to see anyone because she was so frail and she couldn't lift her head up to talk to people. But Ellen said, 'I don't care what she looks like, we'll visit her.' And they sat on the floor, so Isa didn't have to move her head.

Bon's mum was a lovely woman. She knew I loved Bon, and we used to write to each other. I sent her a Christmas card every year until she died in 2011. When she moved into a home, Bon's other brother, Derek, always made sure she got the cards.

Derek has led a very different life to Bon and Graeme. As Bon and Graeme toured the world—Bon with rock bands, Graeme as a merchant seaman—Derek got married and had kids. He didn't really know much about Bon's rock'n'roll life, but now his sons look after Bon's estate.

In 2006, Bon's Scottish hometown, Kirriemuir, held a service to celebrate his life. A message from Vince Lovegrove was read at the event: 'The thing I loved most about Bon Scott was his almost unique self-honesty. What you saw was what you got, he was a real person and as honest as the day is long. To my mind, he was the street poet of my generation and of the generations that followed.'

Kirriemuir has also named a street after Bon—Bon Scott Place—and holds a festival every year called Bonfest. Bon Scott Place is home to a boutique brewery, which has a tasty drop called Big Rosie Lager.

At home, we had two big events in Fremantle in 2008. In February, a bronze statue of Bon was unveiled. The sculptor did a brilliant job, with Bon standing proudly on top of a Marshall amp, microphone in hand.

That weekend, Darce, Gabby and I bumped into The Valentines' first roadie, Mick Christian. This time, he didn't chase Gab with his hammer. Instead, he introduced us to his son. Mick had turned his life around, explaining that getting out of Melbourne was the best thing he'd done. He'd become a lovely bloke. We also met that American producer who was keen to make a movie on Bon's life. I attended a meeting at Alberts about the movie, but without AC/DC's involvement and permission to use the band's music, I don't think a Bon movie will ever make it to the big screen.

A script was actually written. It wasn't too bad, though Darce didn't like some of his character's dialogue—'I've never said "No wukkas" in my life!'—and I thought that an opening sequence of Bon in the shower singing 'Baby, Please Don't Go' into a shampoo bottle was a little too much like a Decore ad. I believe that the movie idea has been shelved and there are now plans to make a documentary on Bon's days in Adelaide with Fraternity and the Mount Lofty Rangers.

I would love to see an AC/DC movie. I reckon Baz Luhrmann would be the man for the job. I envisage a trilogy: the first part would tell the tale of AC/DC's beginnings with Malcolm and Angus; the second instalment would be Bon's story; and then the final part would cover Brian's years with the band.

A few months after the statue was unveiled, we were back in Fremantle for the Bon Scott Letters Exhibition at the Fremantle Arts Centre. We all contributed letters to the event, which opened with a spotlight on a Scottish piper on the roof; it sent chills through the crowd. The mayor then made a speech, praising 'one of our favourite sons'. Graeme had a wry smile. 'You wanted him out of town years ago,' he muttered, as we chuckled to ourselves.

It's funny how things turn out.

In 2003, AC/DC—Bon Scott, Angus Young, Malcolm Young, Cliff Williams, Phil Rudd and Brian Johnson—were inducted into the Rock and Roll Hall of Fame by Aerosmith's Steven Tyler, who praised 'that thunder from Down Under' and spoke of 'the majesty of the power chord'.

He said AC/DC 'lit a fire in the belly of every kid that grew up born to break the rules . . . AC/DC is the ultimate middle-finger aimed at the establishment . . . But just as they reached what seemed to be their creative pinnacle, they experienced the worst kind of tragedy imaginable—the death of the great singer Bon Scott'.

Steve also referred to Angus's school uniform, which he said begged the question: 'How did such big balls get into such small pants?'

To an incredulous American audience, Steve quoted Angus: 'Angus said, "Look, we love to rage on and over the years we put a lot of hard yakka in with our no worries, mate and fuck-all attitude and hair like a bush pig's arse. It's no wonder we had to give a gob-full to a few bloody whingers."'

Steve laughed and said, 'I used to think I didn't understand them because I was fucked up, but it's not just me, right?'

Bon's nephews, Paul and Daniel, accepted the award on Bon's behalf, appearing on stage with the band, including Brian Johnson, who quoted Bon's lyrics to 'Let There Be Rock'.

Steve Tyler spoke of the band's 'journey from the pubs of Australia to the stadiums of the world.

'AC/DC became the litmus test of what rock does. You know, does it make you clench your fist when you sing along? Does it scare your parents to hell and piss off the neighbours? Does it make you dance so close to the fire that you burn your feet and still don't give a rat's arse? Does it make you want to boil your sneakers and make soup out of your girlfriend's panties? If it doesn't, then it ain't AC/DC.'

Epilogue: X marks the memory

A few years ago, a Scottish AC/DC fan arrived in Melbourne and contacted Mary. 'I'll take you around town to where Bon used to live,' Mary said. She took him to The Valentines' old house in Dalgety Street in St Kilda. 'Oh, that's gone,' Mary noted. Next stop was AC/DC's residence in Lansdowne Road, East St Kilda. 'Oh, that's gone, too.'

The buildings might no longer be there, and the times might have changed, but the memories remain.

One of Vince Lovegrove's daughters, Holly, is now writing about her father's life. Vince led a remarkable rock'n'roll life, filled with incredible highs and devastating lows. After The Valentines, Vince worked for *Go-Set* and *RAM*, was a producer for *The Don Lane Show* and worked at radio stations 5KA in Adelaide and 2GB in Sydney. He also managed Cold Chisel and Divinyls. Sadly, Vince's second wife, Suzi, and their son, Troy, both died of AIDS. Vince made ground-breaking documentaries, which helped show the world that AIDS wasn't just a 'gay disease'.

Darce, Gab and Mary attended Vince's sixtieth birthday celebration at a club in Oxford Street, Paddington, in 2007. It was the first time in more than thirty years that The Valentines' old bass player, John Cooksey, had caught up with the other band members. When Vince went to the microphone to make his speech, Cooksey yelled, 'Here comes more bullshit!'

After the official proceedings, Darce, Cooksey and a couple of others went outside for a sly smoke. The venue's bouncer could smell the smoke as it wafted into the club. He confronted the bunch of senior citizens blowing joints: 'Hey, boys,' he smiled, 'ease up, the smoke is blowing up here.'

The Valentines had been busted again.

The party would be the last time they would all see Vince. In March 2012, Vince was killed in a car accident near Byron Bay. His Kombi left the road, rolled and burst into flames. He was sixty-five.

The Valentines' former drummer, Doug Lavery, who had moved back to Australia, had just reconnected with Vince on Facebook. They had arranged to catch up—the week after Vince died.

Bon's brother, Graeme, flew from Thailand for Vince's funeral, in Mullumbimby. Vince had been living nearby in Rosebank, raising his youngest daughter, Lilli. The week after his death, Vince was going to start work as a journalist at *The Northern Star* in Lismore. But he still had the rock'n'roll bug, starting a band called Mongrels of Passion with guitarist Tim Gaze from Tamam Shud and Ariel. Vince loved music. As Chrissy Amphlett noted, 'He had a PhD in rock.'

Darce, Gab and Mary drove to the funeral with Ted and Wyn from The Valentines, Graeme, and their roadie mate, Nicky 'Curly' Campbell. The band, Graeme and the roadies were in the back of the van and Mary in the front, while Gab drove.

It was The Valentines' final gig.

The funeral celebrant asked the mourners to turn off their mobile phones, but halfway through the ceremony, a phone rang, the sound seemingly emanating from the coffin. It was as if Vince were trying to communicate from the great beyond. But Jimmy Barnes's wife, Jane, then discovered she'd left her phone on Vince's coffin.

It was a colourful affair. Vince loved hats, so his friends were encouraged to wear something on their heads. Mary made garlands of flowers, which she and Gab wore in their hair. Vince's daughters, Holly and Lilli, sang Johnny Cash's 'Ring of Fire', a song Vince had been teaching them. And an old Kombi served as the hearse, as the mourners retired to the local RSL, where the rock stars—including Jimmy Barnes, Don Walker and Glenn Shorrock—and roadies told their favourite Vince stories.

Vince had five children to five different women. At his funeral, Peter Head's wife, Mouse, remarked: 'Vince loved women and women loved Vince.' Darce could never work out why, though he admitted, 'You couldn't help but love him.'

Jimmy Barnes had the perfect description of Vince: 'Vince was a passionate man. He was passionate about music, family and friends. He loved life and always threw himself into whatever was before him. I learned a lot from Vince—what to do and what not to do.'

Just three members of The Valentines are still alive. Guitarist Wyn Milson teaches sound production in Sydney; guitarist/bass player Ted Junko is working as a consultant in the building industry in Perth; and Doug Lavery is living in Queensland

and still doing the occasional gig with his old Axiom buddies, Glenn Shorrock and Brian Cadd.

In 2014, Doug went on a train trip to Perth, where he caught up with Ted. They ventured to Fremantle, to have their picture taken with the statue of Bon. Doug remembered the days when they were all starting out in Melbourne, when they were drinking claret and performing on black-and-white TV shows. Then he recalled seeing AC/DC on the 'Highway To Hell' tour in 1979 when he was living in America. Bon called Doug and got him tickets for the band's show at the Long Beach Arena. Doug was struck by AC/DC's power—Bon had come a long way since The Valentines' bubblegum pop.

Bon then spent a couple of days at Doug's place in Newport Beach. Doug was drumming in a local band and they had a gig at a restaurant overlooking the bay. Doug could see Bon sitting at a table at the front of the stage, tapping his fingers in time to the music. Initially, Bon was too shy to get up on stage, 'but we got enough Jack Daniel's in him to get him up'.

Bon sang a few old soul songs, including 'Johnny B. Goode' and 'Good Golly, Miss Molly'. 'No one recognised him, but they loved him,' Doug recalls. 'That's what Bon loved about it—no one knew who he was; he was just having a good time.'

That night in Newport Beach remains Doug's favourite Bon memory, though he also fondly recalls a Valentines gig in Adelaide. 'We were mobbed on stage,' Doug remembers. 'And when we fell down, we broke a lot of stuff, like chairs and tables. It was like a bar fight, except everyone was having fun.'

During their American adventure, Bon and Doug went to a place called Randy's Bar. Bon bought a black T-shirt, which he gave to Mary. She wishes she'd kept it, but she gave it to Randy

Bulpin, the guitarist in Mondo Rock, because she thought he would get a kick out of a T-shirt that said 'Randy's Bar'.

Darce and Gab lost another rock star mate in 2007. Darce got to know Australian guitar great Lobby Loyde in the sixties, before he met The Valentines. Lobby, who'd moved to Melbourne from Brisbane, was playing with Billy Thorpe. As Angry Anderson acknowledged when he inducted Lobby into the ARIA Hall of Fame in 2006, 'More than anyone else, Lobby helped create the Australian guitar sound, long before Angus or Billy Thorpe or The Angels or Rose Tattoo. Lobby inspired Australian bands to step forward and play as loud and aggressively as they could. People are still trying to copy it today.' And it's not just Australian artists—international rock stars, including Kurt Cobain and Henry Rollins, have cited Lobby as an influence.

Lobby was a member of some legendary bands, including The Purple Hearts, Wild Cherries, Billy Thorpe & The Aztecs, The Coloured Balls and Rose Tattoo. And Lobby nearly joined AC/DC. When AC/DC were booked to play at the fourth and final Sunbury Festival in 1975, Angus and Malcolm's older brother, George, was playing bass with the band, as they searched for a new bass player. When George spotted Lobby, he offered him the gig. Murray Engleheart tells the tale in his comprehensive book, *AC/DC: Maximum Rock & Roll*: 'Mate! I know you love playing guitar,' George said to Lobby, 'but this is a fucking great little band and you'd be a killer bass player because you've got the rhythm.' Lobby seriously considered the idea, especially because he was a big fan of drummer Phil Rudd, a former member of The Coloured Balls.

Lobby and Bon were kindred spirits. They never took the limo; they were happiest hanging with the fans and making music. Darce remembers The Purple Hearts reunion, which included a gig at the Woodford Folk Festival. Lobby wandered on stage wearing shorts, a singlet and a pair of slippers. As he rolled a smoke, security appeared, thinking he was an old bum lurking on the stage. As they tried to escort him off the stage, he had to say, 'Hey, I'm playing soon!'

It had Gab thinking of Bon. 'Bon and Lob were very similar people,' she explains. 'They were comfortable in their own skin.'

Gab delivered a eulogy at Lobby's memorial service, laughing when she recounted the story of Lob and Darce going on a road trip to farewell Thorpie, who died just two months before Lobby. 'In the old days,' Gab said, 'they would have been packing trips, grass, speed and jeans and T-shirts. This time it was blood-pressure medication, vitamins, a thermos and their flannelette PJs.'

Everything changes, but some things remain.

The Valentines' old flat on Toorak Road is still there. Every time Darce and Gab drive past they think of how they met. Darce can close his eyes and recall the crazy parties, when people would wander past and witness the mayhem and remark, 'The Valentines are at it again.'

Gab thinks of her childhood friend Betty, the girl who introduced her to the world of rock'n'roll. Sadly, drugs ruined Betty's life. Before she died, she wrote a heartbreaking letter to Gab. 'Don't even try and imagine what it was like,' she said. 'I try hard not to think about the bad times. I love the good times.'

Betty wished she could return to those innocent days when she and Gab were teenagers discovering music for the first time and befriending their favourite band.

'You guys tried so hard to make me see I was mucking up,' Betty continued. 'God I love you. True, I do. I have a true, honest friend in you, Gab.' Betty was living in Orange because she had too many bad memories in Melbourne. She died soon after writing to Gab.

As for Betty's little sister, Judy, Bon's ex-girlfriend, after some wild rock'n'roll years she worked hard to turn her life around, having three beautiful children. Some lives do have a second act.

AC/DC's infamous house in Lansdowne Road was knocked down and replaced by twenty-four apartments. A previous occupant, Vanessa Devereux, placed a plaque at the address:

AC/DC lived here, in a rambling old house in the '70s. I lived here until the house was demolished in 2001. One day I found a plectrum in the garden—was it Angus's? There was also a rubbish pile out the back with lots of bourbon bottles. Empty of course . . . X marks the memory.

After Bon died, Mary and her partner, Peter, realised that life was precious and could be cut short at any time. *Fuck this*, she thought, *let's get married*. Mary and Peter had a son, Paris, and Mary raised Peter's daughter, Erica, as her own. Mary fondly remembers Peter as 'a massive hypochondriac'. Then one day he got sick and died. He had cancer. Peter was also a fabulous artist. He painted a portrait of Bon for Bon's brother, Graeme, who proudly hangs it on his wall and is fascinated by the fact that Bon's eyes seem to follow you no matter which part of the room you're in.

Darce keeps expecting to hear a tap on his bedroom window, then look up to see Bon's cheeky grin. At Vince's sixtieth birthday party, AC/DC bass player Mark Evans asked Darce and Gab: 'Why did Bon never come to your front door? Why did he always have to come through the window?' Darce often thinks about Bon inviting him to London. He is racked with guilt when he thinks of how Bon died, cold and alone in a foreign city. He could have done with a mate.

'Bon might have died alone,' Gab reassures him, 'but that doesn't define how he lived his life.'

Bon was an authentic rock star. He lived his songs. As critic David Fricke noted in the American edition of *Rolling Stone*, Bon sang 'with a lecherous growl that sounded like Tom Waits at 78 rpm, and he was the spitting image of the songs he sang'.

Mary remains in awe of Bon's vocal range. One overseas reviewer said he possessed a 'voice like a weasel on heat'. It's a cool description, but perhaps sells Bon short. He was a vocal chameleon, capable of fitting into whichever band he was fronting, from the sweet, boppy Valentines to the more dramatic rock of Fraternity, and then the raw, rough and ready AC/DC. Has any Australian singer had a more diverse career?

If you really want to know how Bon Scott lived his life, all you need to do is play one of his AC/DC records. As Ted Albert said in his letter to Bon's mum and dad when Bon died, 'Unlike many who pass through life without leaving any trace, Bon has left behind a heritage through his music, records and films [film clips], that will be for the benefit of others for many years to come.'

Darce loves playing AC/DC's second album, *T.N.T.*; invariably, he places the needle on side one, track two, 'Rock'n'roll Singer'. 'It's a great little song,' Darce smiles. It's Bon's defiant declaration. No matter what the world might have had planned for him, he was going to be just one thing: a rock'n'roll star.

Fuck, mate, Darce thinks to himself every time he plays the song, *everything you're singing about there, you fucking did.*

A rock'n'roll singer? Yes, I are!

Occasionally, Mary will click on some old Valentines clips on YouTube and be transported back to the late sixties. Seeing the band's outrageous outfits always brings a smile to her face. The band's very first single, 'Every Day I Have To Cry', remains Mary's favourite Valentines song. 'I don't know why,' she says. 'I guess I just like sad songs.'

Even though Bon confided in Mary that he wanted to settle down, buy a house and maybe start a family, she knew that what he really wanted was to be a rock star. As he cruelly remarked in a *RAM* interview after he joined AC/DC: 'I dug the band more than I dug the chick, so I joined the band and left her.' That throwaway line really hurt Irene. Mary knew Bon didn't mean it—he truly loved Irene—but it showed that rock'n'roll was his top priority.

Bon was always quick with a quip. He told one American interviewer: 'I've never had a message for anyone in my entire life. Except maybe to give out my room number.'

Talking to a Detroit radio station in 1979, he said, 'I was married at the time when I first joined the band and my wife said, "Why don't you write a song about me?" So I wrote "She's Got Balls". Then she divorced me.'

Mary says this story is an example of what she fondly calls 'Bonn-isms'. Bon liked to make a story larger than life and sometimes stretch the truth. Mary doesn't believe the account of Bon going to a maternity ward and visiting two women who were both having his babies, though Bon did one day confide that he'd just been to hospital to visit a woman who had given birth to his baby. 'I'm a dad,' Bon revealed.

And they never talked about it again.

Bon never got to enjoy being a father. 'But he took his songs worldwide,' Darce says. 'And that's all he wanted to do. His dream did come true.'

The only downer was that Bon wasn't around to savour the spoils of success. The seven albums Bon made with AC/DC sold nearly two million copies before he died. Not bad numbers, though most of the proceeds were spent on touring the world, establishing the band. Those seven albums have now sold a combined total of nearly forty million copies.

Mary is proud that her friend is a rock legend, 'but I'd rather he be alive and be less of a legend'.

Bon had so much more to give. As Angus said the month after he died: 'He really hadn't reached his peak.'

'A lot of people sort of think it's sad for us,' Angus added. 'But I think it's more sad for the guy himself, you know, 'cause he always said he would never go unless he was famous. And that's sad for him because just as he was getting somewhere . . .'

Bon will often appear in Mary's dreams. When he first popped up, Mary was confused. 'How come you're alive?' she would ask Bon. 'Where have you been?' The dreams were vivid. But Bon would never tell her. The dreams freaked her out at first, but now she finds them comforting. 'I like to have them, it's like he's still around.'

For Gab, their friend 'is not here, but he is. You see him, but you don't'. She remembers a man who would spend his last few dollars on presents for his friends. She recalls a Christmas when Bon gave their daughter, Bec, a little blue jumper, which Mary had made. While shopping with Bon, Mary picked out her own present—a hat—and Bon bought one for Gab as well. And he presented Darce with a scratch'n'sniff pineapple T-shirt.

Darce worked on many big tours after The Valentines, but he still misses the days when it was 'one band, one van, one roadie'. Being part of a crew of ten meant you had little interaction with the band. Darce yearned for the days of being in the van with the band, hanging out, sharing stories, sharing girls and splitting the money. 'That was magic.'

Darce and Gab's son, Matt, now plays in a band called Rival Fire with John Farnham's son, Robert. Bon's 'Long Way To The Top' is an anthem for them, as it is for every young band. Darce still loves seeing a band in a small room. It has him thinking of the tiny gigs he did with Bon. 'We might have been playing for ten people, but he always played his arse off, and those ten people would tell everyone what they'd missed out on.' Darce highlights a show The Valentines did with Tamam Shud in Sydney. After the local band played, half the crowd left before The Valentines hit the stage. 'But, mate,' Darce smiles, 'they kicked arse. You've got to turn a negative into a positive—that was always Bon's approach.'

In 2007, *Australian Musician* magazine ranked the 50 Most Significant Moments in Australian Pop/Rock. AC/DC's clip for 'It's A Long Way To The Top' came in at number fifteen, with

Ian McFarlane, the author of *The Encyclopedia of Australian Rock and Pop*, calling it 'perfect viewing for the *Countdown* audience who had embraced AC/DC wholeheartedly. It really did capture the essence of the band's working class style, boogie-rock sound and earthy sense of humour.

'And if you want unequivocal proof of the song's continued significance in the history of Australian rock music, you only have to recall the name adopted for the hugely successful 2002 arena rock spectacular: Long Way To The Top.'

Bon's death was at number thirteen, with *Australian Musician* editor, Greg Phillips, writing that 'Bon Scott's legacy will never be forgotten'.

The most significant moment in the first fifty years of Australian rock, according to the *Australian Musician* panel, was 'When Harry Met George'—when Harry Vanda and George Young met at the Villawood migrant hostel in Sydney in 1963. Had this meeting not happened, the magazine argued, 'there would not have been an Easybeats as we know them, possibly no Stevie Wright solo career, certainly not the Albert productions that made AC/DC a huge success'.

Asked what he thought was Australia's greatest music moment, Harry Vanda replied, 'The day Malcolm and Angus asked Bon to be their singer.'

If he'd lived, Bon would now be in his late sixties. 'I know that he'd be young at heart,' Mary says. 'He wouldn't be some boring old guy. I'm not saying he'd be a raving lunatic, but he wouldn't be living a quiet life.'

Mary knows that Bon would still be making music. 'He'd probably have his own little band and they'd be playing up the road from where he lived—when AC/DC weren't touring.'

AC/DC released a boxed set in 1997 as a tribute to Bon. It was called *Bonfire*. The title was inspired by Bon joking about his big dreams: 'When I'm a fucking big shot, I'm calling my solo album "Bonfire".'

Bon is gone, Malcolm can no longer play, and Phil's future with the band is uncertain. Is it still AC/DC?

In the US edition of *Rolling Stone* in 1978, Malcolm Young said he didn't worry about AC/DC becoming too old to rock and roll. He cited Ted Nugent's years on the road before becoming a star. 'Now that he's famous,' Malcolm said, 'he's not gonna get old.'

And that's Bon: forever young. Forever the rock'n'roll rebel with the cheeky grin and the heart of gold.

The memories of Bon keep Mary, Darce and Gab young. As Angus told *Sounds* magazine in 1986, 'Bon joined us pretty late in life, but that guy had more youth in him than people half his age. That was how he thought, and I learned from him. Go out there and be a big kid.'

Two months before his death, Bon told a Scottish interviewer: 'You're never too old to rock'n'roll.'

For many years, Mary would catch up with Bon's ex-wife, Irene, on Bon's birthday, 9 July. They would have a drink for Bon, though nowadays Irene no longer drinks. Now if they don't see each other on the day, they speak on the phone.

On the thirty-fifth anniversary of Bon's death, 19 February 2015, Irene called Mary. 'It's the Bon thing,' Irene said as Mary answered the phone.

'Yeah, I know,' Mary replied. 'I'm eating chocolate.'

Mary keeps to herself on the day of the anniversary, eating junk food, drinking and remembering her friend.

The memory that haunts Mary is the day she and Bon were listening to one of their favourite bands, The Sensational Alex Harvey Band. When his cover of the Jimmie Rodgers' song 'Gamblin' Bar Room Blues' came on, Mary joked to Bon: 'This song reminds me of you!' It's a tale of drinking and dying. Mary can no longer listen to it.

When AC/DC released their *Ballbreaker* album, Malcolm Young told a Melbourne radio interviewer that AC/DC was 'the world's biggest cult band'. Despite their fame and fortune, they 'never became Fleetwood Mac. You don't see us on chat shows or at social parties. We're not so user-friendly. I never jump the queue at the newsagent and I can still enjoy a normal life. I get a lot of double-looks, but they say, "Nah, they're bigger than that." We're short people'.

A framed photo of Bon hangs proudly in Mary's lounge room. Every day it reminds her of the fun they had in Melbourne just weeks before his death. To surprise Bon, Mary took the shot just as he stepped out of the shower; though caught off guard, he's still exhibiting his wicked grin. It's Mary's favourite photo of her friend.

Another image that makes Mary smile is the scene in Cameron Crowe's rock'n'roll movie *Almost Famous* when Stillwater's guitarist Russell Hammond is partying with fans, declaring, 'I am a golden god' as he leaps from a roof into a swimming pool.

'That was Bon,' Mary says. In his shorts and bare feet. 'He was that guy. He wasn't the rock star who went home after the show or hung out with supermodels. He would chat to the fans and say, "Come and have a drink with us."' Searching for something real.

After Bon's death, Angus did an interview with *Sounds* magazine. 'We could be somewhere where you would never expect anyone to know him and someone would walk up and say, "Bon Scott!" and always have a bottle of beer for him.

'Often he would trail off with fans who came backstage after a show and go off with them to a party or something. He judged people as they were and if they invited him and he was in the right mood to go, he went. We used to call him "Bon the Likeable".'

AC/DC bass player Mark Evans tells a funny story about the band's first big gig in London—headlining the Hammersmith Odeon. Bon was late and the rest of the band was freaking out. Bon had refused offers of a limo to the show. And instead of a taxi, he caught a train. And he got on the wrong train. As Mark said in his book, *Dirty Deeds,* 'Seriously, who the fuck catches a train—the wrong fuckin' train no less—to his first headlining gig at the Hammersmith Odeon? Bon Scott, that's who.'

In that same book, Mark referred to Mary as 'Bon's soulmate and companion'.

Angus chuckled when he told Mary that he would never forget Bon's words of advice: 'Bon was always his own person. He would always say to me, "Whatever I do, don't!"'

Mary can still picture that young boy on the high diving board at the Footscray pool. Jumping in at the deep end, floating through the air, grinning at the crowd who had seemingly dared him to jump and then gasped when he actually did.

That was Bon.

'In my mind one of the greatest Australian rock and rollers we've had over the past ten years. I'm talking about the lead singer of AC/DC, Bon Scott. Not only was he a friend of mine, and it shocked me deeply that he died in London, but I think it's a great blow to the Australian industry and especially to AC/DC in the fact that the boys were breaking it so big in Europe and England and were about to become one of the world's top supergroups in the world in 1980.

'The loss of Bon is something that you can't express, because it's something personal within yourself. The only thing I can say is that I've known him for a long, long time. I knew him when he was in The Valentines in the sixties. He's always been one of the greatest showmen I've ever met, he had so much energy, and his loss, well, I just can't . . . I mean, what can you say? Except that we at Countdown, *we owe Bon and the boys a lot—they started off with us.'*

Ian 'Molly' Meldrum on *Countdown*, 24 February 1980

WE SALUTE YOU

Acknowledgements

Mary, Gab and Darce thank Tom Gilliatt, Kathryn Knight, Sarah Baker, Claire de Medici and all at Allen & Unwin.

MARY

Some memories come easy, like it was just yesterday, and others are just too hard to think about. Thank you Jeff Jenkins and Luke Wallis for making this a much easier process than I thought it would be.

Thank you Karen Marks for initiating introductions and telling me, 'Mary, you've got to do this!' And to Serge Thomann for introducing me to Jeff.

To my big brother, Michael: I was the only young girl listening to the Paul Butterfield Blues Band and John Mayall & the Bluesbreakers. Thank you for your early musical influence on me.

Thanks Emma D'Arcy and Nathan Brenner for your help.

Michelle, Pauline, Valerie and mother Violet Dalli . . . 007 loves you.

Margaret Jackson, Karin Paulsen, Christine Sirianni and Heather Johnson: we and our friends lived in weird and wonderful times.

Thank you Gabe James, you went with the ideas I gave you and made them better.

Irene Thornton, you and I have stayed great mates, and I'm sure Bon would love that. We've had lots of laughs and lots of tears; he's always in our hearts. I can picture Bon, up there looking down on us, grinning and thinking, 'How come I never got those two into a threesome?'

Graeme and Lad Scott, Derek and Val Scott—I hope you get lots of enjoyment from this book.

Gabby and Darcy, you darling, crazy couple. We've done it. At last.

My darling children, Paris and Erica, I love you.

And, finally, my beautiful Bon . . . we made a pact: if we were both single in our fifties, we would marry. I think how wonderful your life could have been. You left us much too quickly. I hope there is a Heaven and you're there, living the wonderful and happy life you should have lived down here.

I miss you.

GAB

Betty and I never imagined being grown-ups. I still can't believe that I am!

Bon, Vince, Ted, Wyn, Paddy, Doug and John: thanks for your friendship and love over all these years. Thanks for saying

YES to Darcy when he sought your permission to go out with me! It's a decision that's seen us go through so much together with family and friends for more than forty-five years.

Thanks to my Mum, 'Nin' Lena Fraser, for having faith in Darce and me. And to my sisters and brothers for putting up with a wide-eyed fourteen-year-old who chose a life that was always going to be interesting.

Bec and Matt, thanks for listening to the endless stories, music and crazy ramblings all your lives! Emma and Adrian, too. Emma, a special thanks for your help and guidance getting us on the way with this book.

Thanks to our extended family, friends and my wonderful workmates who have included the hippie D'Arcys in their lives . . . we love you!

Mary, thanks so much for keeping Bon alive. It's your persistence, keeping up with the gossip and all things Bon that's led to us sharing our stories, letters and photos in the Bon Scott Exhibition, AC/DC Family Jewels Exhibition and now this book.

Jeff and Luke, thanks so much for your help and enthusiasm. We've had a ball and could not have done it without you.

Michael Gudinski, thanks for being there for us, from the early days to now. And for being so kind to Lobby.

I wish I could thank Betty today. She knew how much I loved her, and that's all that matters. I miss our old mates; we had the best times together.

Graeme and Lad Scott, thanks for keeping the family connection. It was a long time since you'd seen Bec, but you managed to find her in that bar in Bangkok! We love you guys, as we did your brother.

Scarlett and Mia D'Arcy, by the time you're old enough to read this book, I'm sure you and the rest of the world will still be listening to Bon's songs, and his adoring fans will still be doing graffiti on the corner wall that says:

R.I.P. BON SCOTT

DARCE

Thanks to the following special people: Bon, Paddy, Ted, Wyn, Vince and John. As The Valentines, they gave me a lifetime of experiences in just two years. Experiences that would change my life forever.

Not going with Bon on his journey to England with AC/DC, when he wanted me to be with him, always sat badly with me, as I felt like I had let him down. We both had a tear in our eyes when I said I had to stay with my new family—my wife, Gabby, and daughter, Rebecca. He understood and appreciated my call . . . that was my mate Bon!

I would also like to thank Gab, Mary, Jeff and Luke.

Thanks to all my old roadie mates. B.V.R—One Band, One Van, One Roadie. And all the tour roadies.

To all the bands and great players I was fortunate to work with and hang out with. I cherish every memory.

To my mate Gud, who I have watched over the years build a rock'n'roll empire, which was no easy feat. I'm proud of you, mate! P.S. Thanks for bailing me out of jail!

To my kids: Bec, Matt, Emma, Scarlett, Mia and Adrian—eternal love.

And I'd like to finish with a poem I wrote for all my roadie mates:

WE SALUTE YOU

Old roadies never die
They just move on
To gigs in the sky
Up in the clouds far away
If you listen, you can hear the good ones play

Back on earth they did the miles
Did the gigs
And got the smiles
Blew some numbers
Had a good laugh
With some of the girls you'd have a blast
I wish those days of gigs, girls and grass and long drives
Would always last

We drove the highways
To hit the towns
To keep them up with the latest sounds
From city to city, state to state
They drove and drove to make the date
With lack of food and no sleep
There was a deadline they had to meet

But when we take that long last drive
To be with the ones that were by our side
We cherish what we leave behind
We take it with us in our minds
Love forever, we always say
We'll all be together
There's more gigs to play

Old roadies never die
They just move on to gigs in the sky

RIDE ON

The Bon Scott timeline

1946: Ronald Belford Scott is born in Kirriemuir, Scotland on 9 July. He is the first child of Charles Belford Scott, known as 'Chick', and Isabelle Mitchell, known as 'Isa'.

1949: Bon's brother, Derek, is born.

1952: The Scott family moves to Australia. They live in Sunshine in Melbourne.

1953: Bon's youngest brother, Graeme, is born.

1956: The Scott family moves to Fremantle in Western Australia.

1961: Bon leaves school, aged fifteen.

1964: Bon forms his first band, The Spektors, with guitarist Wyn Milson. Bon is the drummer and occasional lead singer.

1965: The Spektors record some songs for Perth TV show *Club 17*, including covers of Them's 'Gloria', The Beatles' 'Yesterday' and Chuck Berry's 'On My Mind'.

1966: Bon and Wyn team up with Vince Lovegrove, Ted Ward and John Cooksey from fellow Perth band The Winztons to form The Valentines.

1967: The Valentines release their debut single, 'Every Day I Have To Cry' (May). It's a Top 5 hit on the Perth charts.

The Valentines support The Easybeats, featuring George Young, at His Majesty's Theatre in Perth (June).

The Valentines compete in the national final of Hoadley's Battle of the Sounds at Festival Hall in Melbourne, won by The Groop (July).

The Valentines release their second single, 'She Said', written by The Easybeats' Harry Vanda and George Young (August).

The Valentines relocate to Melbourne (October).

1968: The Valentines release their third single, 'I Can Hear The Raindrops' (February).

The Valentines release their fourth single, 'Peculiar Hole In The Sky', written by Vanda and Young (August).

1969: The Valentines release their fifth single, 'My Old Man's A Groovy Old Man', their third written by Vanda and Young (February). It becomes the band's first national hit, peaking at number twenty-three on the *Go-Set* charts.

The Valentines come third in the national final of Hoadley's Battle of the Sounds, won by Doug Parkinson in Focus (July).

The Valentines release their sixth single, 'Nick Nack Paddy Wack' (August), and they're part of 'Operation Starlift', an Australian tour also featuring The Masters Apprentices, Johnny Farnham, Zoot, Johnny Young and Ronnie Burns.

The Valentines are the first Australian band to be arrested for possession of marijuana (September).

1970: Bon writes The Valentines' seventh and final single, 'Juliette' (February). It peaks at number twenty-eight nationally.

The Valentines break up. Bon moves to Sydney and joins Fraternity. He is the band's lead singer and also plays recorder.

Bon plays the recorder on Blackfeather's hit single, 'Seasons of Change'.

1971: Fraternity relocate to Adelaide and release their debut album, *Livestock*. Bon writes one of the songs, 'Raglan's Folly', with guitarist Mick Jurd.

Fraternity play with Deep Purple, Free and Manfred Mann in Adelaide (May).

Fraternity win Hoadley's National Battle of the Sounds, beating Sherbet (August).

Fraternity support Jerry Lee Lewis in Sydney and Adelaide (October).

1972: Bon marries Irene Thornton (24 January).

Fraternity release their second album, *Flaming Galah*.

Fraternity tour the UK.

1973: Still in the UK, Fraternity change their name to Fang and support Geordie, featuring Brian Johnson on lead vocals.

Back in Adelaide, Bon starts singing with The Mount Lofty Rangers, led by Peter Head.

1974: Bon has a motorcycle accident in Adelaide (May). He spends three days in a coma and eighteen days in hospital.

Vince Lovegrove, now running a booking agency, introduces Bon to AC/DC at the Pooraka Hotel in Adelaide. Bon replaces Dave Evans as AC/DC's lead singer (October).

1975: AC/DC release their debut album, *High Voltage* (17 February), produced by Harry Vanda and George Young. Bon writes six of the eight songs with Angus and Malcolm Young: 'She's Got Balls', 'Little Lover', 'Stick Around', 'You Ain't Got A Hold On Me', 'Love Song' and 'Show Business'.

AC/DC enlist a new rhythm section: Phil Rudd on drums and Mark Evans on bass.

Bon dresses as a blonde schoolgirl to perform 'Baby, Please Don't Go' on *Countdown*.

AC/DC release their second album, *T.N.T.* (1 December). Seven of the nine songs were written by Bon, Angus and Malcolm: 'It's A Long Way To The Top (If You Wanna Rock'n'roll)', 'Rock'n'roll Singer', 'The Jack', 'Live Wire', 'T.N.T.', 'Rocker' and 'High Voltage'.

1976: AC/DC film the clip for 'It's A Long Way To The Top (If You Wanna Rock'n'Roll)' on a flat-bed truck in Swanston Street, Melbourne (23 February).

The international edition of *High Voltage* is released, featuring seven songs from *T.N.T.* and two from the original *High Voltage* ('She's Got Balls' and 'Little Lover').

AC/DC's first UK tour (April). Their first gig in England is at The Red Cow in Hammersmith.

AC/DC's third Australian album, *Dirty Deeds Done Dirt Cheap*, is released (20 September). Bon, Angus and Malcolm write all the songs: 'Dirty Deeds Done Dirt Cheap', 'Ain't No Fun (Waiting 'Round To Be A Millionaire)', 'There's Gonna Be Some Rockin'', 'Problem Child', 'Squealer', 'Big Balls', 'R.I.P. (Rock In Peace)', 'Ride On' and 'Jailbreak'.

The international edition of *Dirty Deeds Done Dirt Cheap* is released (17 December), with 'R.I.P. (Rock In Peace)' and 'Jailbreak' replaced by 'Love At First Feel' and *T.N.T.*'s 'Rocker'.

1977: AC/DC release their fourth Australian album, *Let There Be Rock* (21 March), with all songs written by Bon, Angus and Malcolm: 'Go Down', 'Dog Eat Dog', 'Let There Be Rock', 'Bad Boy Boogie', 'Overdose', 'Crabsody In Blue', 'Hell Ain't A Bad Place To Be' and 'Whole Lotta Rosie'.

Bon and Irene divorce (7 March).

Mark Evans leaves AC/DC, replaced by Englishman Cliff Williams.

AC/DC perform their first American show, at Armadillo World Headquarters in Austin, Texas (27 July).

Let There Be Rock becomes AC/DC's first charting album in the UK, peaking at number seventeen. It reaches number 154 in the US.

1978: AC/DC release their fifth Australian album, *Powerage* (5 May), with all songs written by Bon, Angus and Malcolm: 'Rock'n'roll Damnation', 'Down Payment Blues', 'Gimme A Bullet', 'Riff Raff', 'Sin City', 'What's Next To The Moon', 'Gone Shootin'',

'Up To My Neck In You' and 'Kicked In The Teeth'. It is the last AC/DC studio album with Bon produced by Vanda and Young. It reaches number twenty-six in the UK, and 133 in the US.

AC/DC score their first Top 40 single in the UK, with 'Rock'n'Roll Damnation' hitting number twenty-four (10 June).

AC/DC release their first live album, *If You Want Blood You've Got It*. It is the last Bon album to be produced by Vanda and Young.

Powerage peaks at number twenty-six in the UK, followed by *If You Want Blood You've Got It*, which reaches number thirteen.

1979: AC/DC's sixth Australian album, *Highway To Hell*, is released (27 July). Produced by Mutt Lange, all songs are written by Bon, Angus and Malcolm: 'Highway To Hell', 'Girls Got Rhythm', 'Walk All Over You', 'Touch Too Much', 'Beating Around The Bush', 'Shot Down In Flames', 'Get It Hot', 'If You Want Blood (You've Got It)', 'Love Hungry Man' and 'Night Prowler'. It is the band's first album to crack the US Top 100.

1980: Bon makes his final TV appearance, performing *Highway To Hell*'s 'Touch Too Much' on *Top Of The Pops* in the UK (7 February).

Bon Scott is found dead in a car in East Dulwich, South London, after a night drinking (19 February). The death certificate lists the official cause of death as 'acute alcoholic poisoning'. Bon is thirty-three.

Bon is buried at the Fremantle Cemetery.

Brian Johnson, ex-Geordie, becomes AC/DC's new lead singer (1 April).

AC/DC release *Back In Black* (25 July). It enters the UK charts at number one, and goes on to become one of the ten biggest-selling albums of all time worldwide.

The live concert movie *AC/DC: Let There Be Rock* hits cinemas (September). It was filmed on 9 December 1979 at the Pavillon de Paris in France.

1988: AC/DC are among the first inductees into the ARIA Hall of Fame.

1994: Clinton Walker releases his Bon biography, *Highway to Hell: The life and death of AC/DC legend Bon Scott.*

1997: AC/DC release the boxed set *Bonfire* as a tribute to Bon (17 November).

1999: Bon's dad, Chick, dies, aged eighty-one.

2003: Bon is inducted into the Rock and Roll Hall of Fame as a member of AC/DC.

2004: *Classic Rock* magazine places Bon at number one in its list of the '100 Greatest Frontmen Of All Time'.

The Australian movie *Thunderstruck*, starring Stephen Curry, Damon Gameau and Sam Worthington, tells the story of a group of AC/DC fans making a pilgrimage to Bon's grave.

Melbourne's Corporation Lane is renamed AC/DC Lane (1 October). Lord Mayor John So says: 'As the song says, there is a highway to hell, but this is a laneway to heaven. Let us rock.'

2005: Bon is inducted into the WAMi (Western Australian Music Industry) Hall of Fame.

The National Trust lists Bon's grave as a Heritage and Cultural Icon.

2008: A Bon Scott statue is unveiled in Fremantle.

2011: Bon's mum, Isa, dies, aged ninety-four.

A stage show, *Hell Ain't a Bad Place to Be: The Story of Bon Scott*, opens in Melbourne, starring Nick Barker and Doug Parkinson, and directed by Brian Nankervis.

Mark Evans releases his autobiography, *Dirty Deeds*, the first AC/DC book written by an AC/DC member.

2012: AC/DC's catalogue becomes available on iTunes (19 November).

2014: Bon's former wife, Irene Thornton, releases a book, *My Bon Scott.*